Treatment for Children with Selectiv

MW00807320

EDITOR-IN-CHIEF

David H. Barlow, PhD

SCIENTIFIC
ADVISORY BOARD

Anne Marie Albano, PhD

Gillian Butler, PhD

David M. Clark, PhD

Edna B. Foa, PhD

Paul J. Frick, PhD

Jack M. Gorman, MD

Kirk Heilbrun, PhD

Robert J. McMahon, PhD

Peter E. Nathan, PhD

Christine Maguth Nezu, PhD

Matthew K. Nock, PhD

Paul Salkovskis, PhD

Bonnie Spring, PhD

Gail Steketee, PhD

John R. Weisz, PhD

G. Terence Wilson, PhD

✓ **Programs** *That Work*™

Treatment for Children with Selective Mutism

An Integrative Behavioral Approach

R. Lindsey Bergman

OXFORD
UNIVERSITY PRESS

OXFORD
UNIVERSITY PRESS

Oxford University Press is a department of the University of Oxford.
It furthers the University's objective of excellence in research, scholarship,
and education by publishing worldwide.

Oxford   New York
Auckland   Cape Town   Dar es Salaam   Hong Kong   Karachi
Kuala Lumpur   Madrid   Melbourne   Mexico City   Nairobi
New Delhi   Shanghai   Taipei   Toronto

With offices in
Argentina   Austria   Brazil   Chile   Czech Republic   France   Greece
Guatemala   Hungary   Italy   Japan   Poland   Portugal   Singapore
South Korea   Switzerland   Thailand   Turkey   Ukraine   Vietnam

Oxford is a registered trademark of Oxford University Press in the UK and certain other
countries.

Published in the United States of America by
Oxford University Press
198 Madison Avenue, New York, NY 10016

© R. Lindsey Bergman 2013

All rights reserved. No part of this publication may be reproduced, stored in a
retrieval system, or transmitted, in any form or by any means, without the prior
permission in writing of Oxford University Press, or as expressly permitted by law,
by license, or under terms agreed with the appropriate reproduction rights organization.
Inquiries concerning reproduction outside the scope of the above should be sent to the
Rights Department, Oxford University Press, at the address above.

You must not circulate this work in any other form
and you must impose this same condition on any acquirer.

Library of Congress Cataloging-in-Publication Data

Bergman, R. Lindsey.
Treatment for children with selective mutism: an integrative behavioral approach/R. Lindsey Bergman.
p. cm. — (Programs that work)
Includes bibliographical references.
ISBN 978–0–19–539152–7 (pbk.)
1. Selective mutism—Treatment.   2. Cognitive therapy.   I. Title.
RJ506.M87B47 2012
616.89'1425—dc23
2012024763

About Programs *ThatWork*™

Stunning developments in healthcare have taken place over the last several years, but many of our widely accepted interventions and strategies in mental health and behavioral medicine have been brought into question by research evidence as not only lacking benefit, but perhaps inducing harm. Other strategies have been proven effective using the best current standards of evidence, resulting in broad-based recommendations to make these practices more available to the public. Several recent developments are behind this revolution. First, we have arrived at a much deeper understanding of pathology, both psychological and physical, which has led to the development of new, more precisely targeted interventions. Second, our research methodologies have improved substantially, such that we have reduced threats to internal and external validity, making the outcomes more directly applicable to clinical situations. Third, governments around the world and healthcare systems and policymakers have decided that the quality of care should improve, that it should be evidence based, and that it is in the public's interest to ensure that this happens (Barlow, 2004; Institute of Medicine, 2001).

Of course, the major stumbling block for clinicians everywhere is the accessibility of newly developed evidence-based psychological interventions. Workshops and books can go only so far in acquainting responsible and conscientious practitioners with the latest behavioral healthcare practices and their applicability to individual patients. This new series, Programs *ThatWork*™, is devoted to communicating these exciting new interventions to clinicians on the front lines of practice.

The manuals and workbooks in this series contain step-by-step detailed procedures for assessing and treating specific problems and diagnoses. But this series also goes beyond the books and manuals by providing ancillary materials that will approximate the supervisory process in assisting practitioners in the implementation of these procedures in their practice.

In our emerging healthcare system, the growing consensus is that evidence-based practice offers the most responsible course of action for the mental health professional. All behavioral healthcare clinicians deeply desire to provide the best possible care for their patients. In this series, our aim is to close the dissemination and information gap and make that possible.

This therapist guide addresses the treatment of selective mutism (SM) in young children. SM is an impairing behavioral condition in which a child does not speak in certain social situations despite speaking regularly and normally in other situations. The onset of SM is usually early, during the preschool years, and impairment is significant because youth do not typically "grow out of it" and start speaking in school. Selective mutism impacts children's social, emotional, and academic functioning during a critical time in their development. Though SM is related to social phobia, it cannot be treated in the same way because of the young age of those affected, their lack of speech in a treatment setting, and the need for school involvement in the treatment.

The approach developed by Dr. R. Lindsey Bergman and outlined in this guide integrates input from the clinician, parents, teacher, and others impacted by the child's lack of speech. It utilizes exposure exercises and behavioral interventions that target gradual increases in speaking across settings in which the child has difficulty. Techniques such as stimulus fading, shaping, and systematic desensitization are combined and used flexibly with a behavioral reward system to allow for a gradual exposure to speaking situations.

This effective, empirically supported treatment protocol for SM will be invaluable to clinicians who wish to use a comprehensive, individualized program to help children with SM and their families.

David H. Barlow, Editor-in-Chief,
Programs *That Work*™
Boston, MA

References

Barlow, D. H. (2004). Psychological treatments. *American Psychologist, 59,* 869–878.

Institute of Medicine. (2001). *Crossing the quality chasm: A new health system for the 21st century.* Washington, DC: National Academy Press.

Contents

Acknowledgments

Thank you to John Piacentini, PhD, Melody Keller, PhD, Lisa O'Malley, MA, Araceli Gonzalez, PhD, and Lindsey Hunt who have helped with the development of this treatment over many years, and to all of the children, families, and therapists who shared their thoughts and gave feedback crucial to the development and implementation of this manual.

Treatment for Children with Selective Mutism

Chapter 1 *Introductory Information for Therapists*

Background Information and Purpose of This Program

This manual describes a multicomponent outpatient treatment program for children ages 4–8 years with selective mutism (SM). Selective mutism is an impairing behavioral condition in which a child fails to speak in certain social situations despite speaking regularly and normally in other situations. Although SM is closely related to childhood social phobia, the existing cognitive behavioral treatments that are effective for social phobia are often not appropriate for the treatment of SM. The frequent failure of children with SM to speak to the therapist (at least during early sessions), the typically young age of children with SM, and the need for considerable involvement of school personnel (usually teachers) are the most noteworthy reasons that necessitate modification of existing cognitive behavioral therapy (CBT) protocols.

This treatment approach emphasizes behavioral techniques to be used in conjunction with exposure-based intervention. Due to the limited cognitive development of young children, the use of cognitive strategies is restricted to rather simple techniques. Although these techniques are described within specific session chapters, they should be utilized when appropriate. Similarly, it should be noted that treatment in general may not always proceed at the pace that is outlined in the manual. Rather, some children may advance through the sessions at a faster pace and, others may require more time to proceed through treatment. In addition, specific interventions or exposures are included in this guide as instructive or illustrative examples, but they by no means comprise an exhaustive inventory of techniques to be utilized. Creativity in designing interventions is crucial and therapists should avoid overreliance on the suggested interventions in the manual. Doing so would likely curtail or limit the development of unique and individualized interventions.

This manual outlines the sequence and required components of the standard treatment procedures and activities of our SM program for children. Although the manual contains sample dialogues, the actual level of presentation may vary depending on the age and developmental level of the child. As such, the wording of the examples in this manual is illustrative; however, it is recommended that therapists closely follow dialogues set in italics. Given that the treatment was developed for children ages 4–8 years, the most typical adaptation will be for older children who are capable of more abstract thinking as well as a more collaborative approach. Although therapists should use clinical experience and judgment when determining the presentation level and complexity of treatment for a given child, ideas regarding adaptation for the older child are presented in Chapter 13, Additional Treatment Considerations.

Disorder or Problem Focus

Selective mutism is considered to be an impairing condition that interferes with both educational achievement and socialization (e.g., Bergman, Piacentini, & McCracken, 2002; Black & Uhde, 1995; Dummit, Klein, Tancer, Asche, & Martin, 1997). Recent evidence indicates that SM may be more prevalent than previously believed, with rates as high as 0.7–0.8% (Bergman et al., 2002; Elizur & Perednik, 2003), only slightly less than those of other childhood psychiatric disorders (e.g., obsessive-compulsive disorder). The primary symptom of SM is, of course, failure to speak despite the presence of normal speaking ability. The lack of speech tends to be affected by several variables including setting, individuals present, and situation. Normal speech must be present in at least one situation or setting, and the home environment is almost always the setting in which speech is present. In fact, a complete lack of speech at home is reason to suspect a diagnosis other than SM.

Selective mutism presents a significant mental and public health problem due to its impact on the social, emotional, and academic functioning of young children at a critical point in their development. The prevalence of SM is higher than previously thought, and data indicates that the lack of speech interferes with education and socialization. These factors, along with the relative lack of knowledge of the disorder among teachers, school officials, and even mental health practitioners, indicate the need increased awareness, and the validation of effective treatments.

Comorbidity

SM is presumed to be closely related to social anxiety disorder, with most researchers finding comorbidity rates well above 50% (e.g., Manassis, Tannock, Garland, Minde, & McInnes, 2007; Vecchio & Kearney, 2005). Therefore, it is not surprising that most children with SM appear behaviorally inhibited; however, a small number of children with SM present without social anxiety. These children may greet new people with a broad smile, bold nonverbal gestures, and no hint of shyness. In their recent review, Viana, Beidel, and Rabian (2009) discuss the association of SM with many additional disorders including other anxiety disorders, communication and developmental disorders or delays, language and speech disorders, and elimination disorders. However, large, well-designed studies investigating the presence of these disorders among children with SM are lacking.

There are somewhat conflicting and confusing data regarding whether children with SM may also have oppositional or defiant tendencies (see Viana et al., 2009 for discussion). Regardless of whether this is the case, clinicians and family members should take care not to mistake anxiety-related resistance to speak for generalized defiance. Assessing the presence of defiant behavior in other areas of life (or whether it appears only in situations related to speaking or social interaction) can be helpful in establishing whether oppositionality is a defining or significant feature of the child's psychiatric picture.

Prognosis

Due to the fact that there are no relevant prospective longitudinal studies, very little is known about the long-term course of SM. There are some data indicating symptom improvement, but not remission, among children in grades K–2 over a 6-month period (Bergman et al., 2002). Interestingly, adults identified as having had SM as children retrospectively report that the SM remits but that social anxiety and significant avoidance behaviors continue (Dow, Sonies, Scheib, Moss, & Leonard, 1995; Steinhausen, Wachter, Laimbock, & Metzke, 2006).

Diagnostic Criteria for SM

For a diagnosis of SM, the criteria from the text revision of the *Diagnostic and Statistical Manual of Mental Disorders, Fourth Edition* must be met as follows:

A. Consistent failure to speak in specific social situations (in which there is an expectation for speaking; e.g., at school) despite speaking in other situations.

B. The disturbance interferes with educational or occupational achievement or with social communication.

C. The duration of the disturbance is at least 1 month (not limited to the first month of school).

D. The failure to speak is not due to a lack of knowledge of, or comfort with, the spoken language required in the social situation.

E. The disturbance is not better accounted by a communication disorder (e.g., stuttering) and does not occur exclusively during the course of a pervasive developmental disorder, schizophrenia, or other psychotic disorder.

Development of This Treatment Program and Evidence Base

Despite growing interest in the phenomenology of SM, well-designed treatment studies remain lacking. At present, there are no controlled trials of psychosocial treatment, nor are empirically supported treatment protocols specifically for SM available. To begin to remedy this lack, we have developed and provided preliminary evidence for the effectiveness of a SM treatment. Our approach addresses SM in an innovative manner by employing an interdisciplinary transfer of control model (Silverman & Kurtines, 1996) that (a) trains parents to effectively drive treatment beyond the acute clinic intervention and (b) includes teachers in the treatment process and helps them develop the necessary skills to address SM symptomatology, both at the acute level and beyond.

Previous Studies

Published data on the treatment of SM are typically limited to single case studies and case series of markedly varying quality. Much of this treatment literature does not identify diagnostic procedures, assessment or outcome methods, number of treatment sessions, or details of the treatment method. These inadequacies, along with the lack of controlled trials, make it difficult to assess treatment efficacy or replicate described treatments. In spite of these weaknesses, the conviction that behavioral techniques are an essential component to the treatment of SM is wide-spread (e.g., Cohan, Chavira, & Stein, 2006; Kearney, Haight, & Day, 2011). Furthermore, studies that did utilize adequate methodological methods support such behavioral techniques for treatment of SM (e.g., Vecchio & Kearney, 2009). What is clearly lacking in the published literature on treatment of SM are manualized treatments similar to those for treatment of other anxiety-related childhood disorders (e.g., Kendall, 1994; Kendall & Hedtke, 2006; Piacentini, Langley, & Roblek, 2007).

Among the case studies and series are many reports of successful treatment focused on the application of several behavioral techniques aimed at increasing speech production where it is lacking. Published reports describe the use of behavioral techniques such as contingency management (Masten, Stacks, Caldwell-Colbert, & Jackson, 1996; Vecchio & Kearney, 2009), stimulus fading (Richburg & Cobia, 1994), systematic desensitization (Rye & Ullman, 1999), negative reinforcement (Krohn, Weckstein, & Wright, 1992), and shaping (Watson & Kramer, 1992; Porjes, 1992). Notably, several reports describe treatments utilizing somewhat unique self-modeling behavioral interventions involving audio (Blum et al., 1998) and video (Lang, Regester, Mulloy, Rispoli, & Botout, 2011) editing techniques. As is often noted (e.g., Bergman &

Lee, 2009; Cohan, et al, 2006), a combination of behavioral techniques is the most common and successful treatment approach. Interestingly, results from a recent well-designed open treatment trial (Vecchio & Kearney, 2009) suggest that both exposure-based techniques and parent contingency management are effective in the treatment of SM, though the exposure-based treatment appears somewhat more beneficial. It is noteworthy that although there are two fairly distinct literatures regarding treatment for SM—one characterized by the discipline of educational psychology (e.g., Cleave, 2009) and the other within the realm of clinical psychology—both focus primarily on behavioral techniques.

Development of Standardized Treatment for SM

As noted earlier, although there are well-developed and empirically validated manualized treatments for other childhood anxiety-related disorders, there are no currently available manualized treatment protocols for SM. Although SM appears to be closely related to child anxiety, the extant treatments for child anxiety require significant modification to improve their suitability for treatment of SM. The factors that contribute to the need for modification to existing treatment protocols include the child's failure to speak, the young age of most SM patients, and the need for significant school involvement in almost all cases. The manualized behavioral treatment presented in this guide addresses these factors and is supported by preliminary evidence.

The treatment approach that serves as the basis of the current manual was developed over the past several years by Dr. Bergman as part of the UCLA Childhood OCD, Anxiety, and Tic Disorders Program. The first SM child was evaluated in 1998, and to date approximately 90 children have received treatment in our clinical program. We began to systematize our approach to the treatment of SM in 2000 with the use of an integrated behavioral approach that was administered in a consistent manner to all child participants. As part of our systematic approach to treatment delivery, clinicians routinely assigned Clinical Global Impression scores for both Improvement and Severity (CGI-I, CGI-S; Guy, 1976) at each treatment session. The CGI-I data from the clinical sample ($n = 75$) suggest that, on average, significant clinical improvement was achieved by Session 20 of the behavioral treatment course.

In addition to this improvement, a paired sample t-test revealed a significant decrease in CGI-S (Guy, 1976) ratings from baseline ($X = 4.46$, $SD = .66$) to Treatment Session 8 ($X = 3.81$, $SD = .48$), $t (1, 12) = 3.16$, $p = .008$. Although this change is statistically significant, we consider it important to note that the average clinician CGI-S at Session 8 remains indicative of a clinical disorder (CGI of 4 = moderately ill). However, the average CGI-S available for later in treatment (between Sessions 20 and 30, $M = 26$, $SD = 2.68$) had decreased to 2.58 ($SD = 1.08$), $t (1, 11) = 6.63$, $p < .001$ (CGI-S of 2 = borderline ill; CGI-S of 3 = mildly ill).

Following several years of experience with the open treatment of children with SM using the developed behavioral treatment, we secured funding from the National Institutes of Health to manualize and test the efficacy of the treatment approach. The resulting manual, entitled *Integrated Behavioral Treatment for Selective Mutism* (unpublished manual), was first piloted with several children and then tested in a small, randomized, controlled study of 21 children ages 4–8 years. Twelve children were randomized to and completed 20 sessions of active treatment and 9 children were assigned to a 12-week waitlist control condition. Although it would be methodologically preferable to match the lengths of the two conditions, we were ethically bound to limit the waiting list to 12 weeks due to the impairing nature of the condition. Children who participated in this treatment study met diagnostic criteria for SM as their primary diagnosis and were not on psychotropic medication. Ninety-five percent of the children additionally met criteria for a diagnosis of social phobia, as is common among children with SM. Doctoral-level psychology students who were well familiarized with CBT for children administered the treatment under close supervision. To address the lack of speech at school, the treatment focused on the assignment of school-based assignment exercises. To ensure that children would have the opportunity to accomplish these tasks, all children enrolled in the study were required to be regularly attending school 5 days per week or, if during summer, to be enrolled in day camp or regular structured group activities with peers at least 3 days per week.

An independent evaluator (IE) who was unaware of the child's treatment status administered the Anxiety Disorder Interview Schedule (Silverman

& Albano, 1996) following the conclusion of the assigned condition (24 weeks for active, 12 weeks for waitlist). Based on the results of the interview, 8 children (67% response rate) in the active treatment group did not meet criteria for selective mutism at the end of the treatment period. All children in the waitlist condition continued to meet diagnostic criteria for SM at conclusion of the waitlist period. The difference between treatment response for active treatment versus waitlist was significant, $\chi 2(1, N = 21) = 9.70, p = .002$. Examining response status in terms of the IE-designated CGI-I score also indicated a robust response to treatment, in that 75% of the children randomized to active treatment received CGI-I scores of 2 or above (indicating at least "much better") and none of the children in the waiting list condition received ratings reaching this response criterion. Chi-square analysis revealed the difference in CGI-I scores to be significant, $\chi 2(1, N = 21) = 11.81, p <.001$.

Model of SM and Behavioral Therapy

The behavioral conceptualization of SM (see Figure 1.1) and the resulting treatment model focus on the expectation of speaking in certain situations as a trigger for an increase in anxiety. The response to increased anxiety is avoidance of speech that then serves to reduce the anxiety. Avoidance is negatively reinforced over time when it is successful in reducing the anxiety that was triggered by the expectation of speech. For example, a child with SM may become anxious when the teacher asks her a question. The child's anxiety increases as the teacher and class wait for her to answer and she herself attempts to answer. The anxiety will likely cause the child with SM to avoid answering the question, and her avoidance may successfully result in a decrease in anxiety. The reduction in anxiety then reinforces the avoidance, thus strengthening the symptom pattern.

Behavioral exposure therapy consists of gradually exposing the child with SM to situations in which speech is expected. Then, the child's capacity to speak is facilitated while their response pattern of avoidance is discouraged. The success of the program is based largely on the principle of beginning with a task that is easy and nonthreatening enough for the

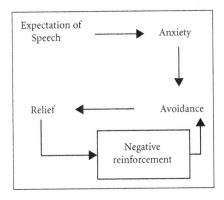

Figure 1.1

Behavioral conceptualization of selective mutism

child to tolerate. When the child successfully completes this early "easy" exposure instead of avoiding the speech or approximation of speech, she is able to break the cycle of negative reinforcement, and instead, the desired behavior (speech) is positively reinforced. Thus begins the process of gradually increasing the difficulty of the speaking situations that are presented to the child with the expectation that speech will be produced.

Risks and Benefits of This Treatment Program

We have found no adverse effects associated with the use of behavioral therapy for SM. Participation in exposure exercises, however, may temporarily increase a child's anxiety and children do often become distressed. Tears are not uncommon, but are usually short lived. We recommend that clinical judgment be utilized in determining when to modify an exercise so that it is less demanding and distressing, and when to continue to urge a child to complete the original exercise. Similarly, parents should receive some training on this issue. Some parents find the time-intensive nature of this treatment to be logistically difficult and may prefer medication treatment, as it requires less time commitment. On the other hand, children presenting for treatment of SM are typically quite young and their parents often prefer to avoid the use of psychotropic medication.

Alternative Treatments

As noted and described earlier, of the various psychosocial treatment modalities, behavioral intervention is the most routinely recognized as effective for selective mutism despite a lack of quality empirical investigation in the area. Other interventions such as play therapy, art therapy, and language therapy, tended to be used as treatments for SM more commonly in the past. When these treatment efforts were published, information regarding diagnostic procedures, treatment methods, standardized measurements, and the like was insufficient to evaluate their merit. More recently, some attempts to deliver behavioral treatment within the group setting appear to be effective (e.g., Sharkey, McNicholas, Barry, Begley, & Ahearn, 2008). The role of medication as an alternative treatment is discussed in the next section.

The Role of Medications

There is no reason to exclude children who are taking medication for SM from this treatment program. Furthermore, no modifications to the treatment approach are necessary for children who are concurrently taking medication. If a child who previously experienced symptoms of SM is taking medication and is currently asymptomatic, this treatment program can be initiated if symptoms return upon discontinuation of medication. At present, there have been no studies testing the treatment program against medication.

As Carlson et al. (2008) notes in his review of 21 studies of medication treatment of SM, most studies have significant methodological limitations. For example, 81% of the studies in the literature are case studies, and only one of these studies reported on the use of standardized instruments to measure change (Wright, Cuccaro, Leonhardt, Kendall, & Anderson, 1995). There were two medication trials using fluoxetine in the 1990s: a double-blind placebo-controlled study (Black & Uhde, 1994), and an open trial (Dummit et al., 1996). The results of these were mixed but did provide support for the use of selective serotonin reuptake inhibitor (SSRI) medication for the treatment of SM, which is not surprising given that there is considerable empirical support for the treatment of social anxiety among youth with SSRIs (e.g., The Research Unit on Pediatric Psychopharmacology Anxiety Study Group, 2001). Recently, Manassis and Tannock (2008) examined follow-up data that suggested that children with SM who received treatment with SSRI medication showed significant symptoms improvement over a 6- to 8-month period.

Outline of This Treatment Program

The treatment protocol consists of 20 sessions, 60 minutes each, delivered over the course of 24 weeks. The first 18 sessions are delivered weekly with 2-week intervals between the last two sessions in order to foster increased generalizability and to promote transfer of control and a smoother termination. As SM is often school related, it is much preferred for this treatment to be undertaken during the school year, so that the child is able to practice and increase her comfort speaking in the environment with which she is having trouble. If a family comes in for treatment during the summer, it is essential that the child be involved in a structured daily program (e.g., camp) and, if at all possible, at a camp that takes place at the child's school.

Integrated Behavioral Therapy

This approach utilizes many standard behavioral interventions targeting gradual increases in appropriate speaking behaviors across settings in which the child initially has difficulties speaking. When the child remains in the anxiety-provoking situations (i.e., those requiring speech) and successfully speaks rather than avoiding speech, habituation to speaking-related anxiety occurs and speaking can be positively reinforced. The integrated nature of the therapy refers to the goal of integrating input from the clinician with that from the parents and teacher (as well as others impacted by the lack of speech). Together these individuals form a treatment team that constructs and implements exposure assignments.

Hierarchy/Talking Ladder

At the beginning stages of treatment, the treatment team (including the child) constructs a list of situations and settings in which the child has difficulty speaking. With help, the child "rates" these situations (including individuals spoken to within these situations) in terms of how difficult speech would be, and these ratings determine the order in which speaking assignments are made. The situations are assigned in a graduated fashion ("easiest" first) to maximize the chance of habituation and initial treatment success. If a given exposure is more difficult than anticipated, and a child is very distressed (e.g., crying), an easier exposure is instead attempted, or the exposure is modified to make it less difficult. Initially, assignments tend to be contained within the clinic setting (simulated if necessary), and then transitioned to school-based exposures. In general, the highest priority should be placed on school-based work because school tends to be the site of the greatest functional impairment among children with SM.

In most cases, the most important function of the hierarchy will be to help the therapist identify an appropriate starting place for exposure exercises. As treatment progresses, the ratings on the hierarchy may quickly become obsolete. The therapist can either work with the family to rerate items on the hierarchy or just continue to work on the items in their original order without attention to difficulty ratings. In general, the hierarchy serves as a template or guide for exposures but not a hard-and-fast instruction that must be followed. The therapist should also beware that young children may be quite inaccurate in their ratings of what will or will not be difficult.

Exposure Exercises

Exposure exercises are based on traditional behavioral techniques such as stimulus fading, shaping, and systematic desensitization, which also allow gradual exposure to the speaking situation. These techniques are usually combined and used flexibly with a behavioral reward system that allow children to earn toys, social outings, and privileges for participation in treatment. Once the child is informed that they will earn a specific reward for a specific behavior, it is of the utmost importance that there is unequivocal follow-through. The child should get what was promised if, and only if, they do what was assigned. Notably, treatment may also include somewhat unique self-modeling behavioral interventions using audio and possibly video editing techniques (e.g., Lang, Regester, Mulloy, Rispoli, & Botout, 2011) and computerized interactive software (e.g., the Dr. Speech program; http://www.drspeech.com/index.html).

The construction of exposure exercises is at the core of this treatment. A great deal of skill, creativity, and ingenuity goes into this individualized process. As such, specific exposure exercises are not described in a session-by-session manner in this manual. Instead, an illustrative list of behavioral exposure techniques is included in Appendix A. This list is by no means exhaustive; there are as many viable exposure exercises are there are children and therapists. In general, we follow a principle of repeating the use of successful behavioral exposures and/or specific techniques/interventions in different settings or at different levels of the child's hierarchy. For example, if a child first spoke to the therapist when allowing the therapist to slowly enter and join the game while the child played hangman with a parent, the child would then attempt to play hangman with a parent and have the teacher slowly enter and join the game. When possible, exposure situations that contain inherent rewards should be used: for example, asking for an ice cream at an ice cream shop (ice cream is the reward). For at-home exposure assignments, it is important to keep abreast of events in the child's life so as to use these real-life happenings in the treatment (e.g., "Play 'guess who' with your cousin" when the child's cousin is in town visiting).

Opportunites for exposures during session may present themselves in the surroundings of the therapy office. With a parent's permission, and understanding that others will probably realize that that the child is undergoing treatment, it can be quite useful to utilize others in an office suite, office building (i.e., doorman, strangers, etc.) in the surrounding environment.

Parental Participation

Active parental participation is an absolutely vital component of the successful treatment of SM in young children. Parents are almost always part of sessions for review of exposure assignments and explanation and planning of future assignments. Their participation in the remainder of the session will vary according to the child's individual symptom profile and the phase of treatment. Out of session, most of the responsibility for planning and execution of exposure assignments lies with the parent. Specifically, parents will be responsible for treatment-related activities such as organizing play dates, scheduling exposures with teachers, providing opportunities for the child to order in a restaurant, and so forth. Last, parents provide invaluable input regarding their child's behavior in a variety of situations. At the beginning of treatment, parents will receive psychoeducation regarding selective mutism as well as information on behavioral techniques and the treatment protocol.

Teacher Participation

Likewise, teacher participation is virtually always an essential component because school is the most common setting for SM symptoms to be present. As such, the therapist typically requires information from the teacher to best understand the child's individual patterns of speaking in the classroom. This information will help in devising speaking assignments within the classroom. In addition, the teacher is asked to participate in short speaking assignments on a weekly basis. These usually require 10–20 minutes per week and are communicated to the teacher via assignment forms or a notebook completed in session and delivered by the parent. The teacher will typically need to prompt or remind the child to do simple tasks, and others may be scheduled in advance. Initially, the therapist should plan at least an initial telephone conversation with the teacher for introductions.

Transfer of Control

Although input from everyone involved is always encouraged, during the initial phase of treatment the therapist takes primary responsibility for directing most aspects of the treatment, especially exposure assignments. One of the guiding principles of the treatment is that this responsibility or "control" should be gradually transferred to parents and teachers, and, to the extent possible, to the child. Although the attempt to transfer control to parents and teachers is a vital component throughout the treatment, it becomes most important as formal treatment nears an end. Increasing parents and teachers' responsibility for the intervention will facilitate their mastery of treatment principles and capability of continuing elements of treatment. This is essential; although children with SM are quite likely to show significant improvement by Session 20, some may remain reluctant to speak in certain situations and will benefit from additional behavioral exposure exercises planned and facilitated by parents and teachers.

During the last two or three sessions, the respective roles of parent(s) and therapist should undergo a shift. That is, instead of the therapist leading the process, parents, with supervision from the therapist, will take the lead in the child's treatment. They will take the primary responsibility for devising and assigning speaking tasks, revising tasks (if necessary), setting goals, managing behavioral reward system, and the like. The therapist will provide feedback regarding the execution of these tasks and will attempt to shape parents' skills. From our previous experience, we believe that parents are quite capable of fulfilling these responsibilities and that most of them naturally progress toward a substantial role in the process by the end of treatment.

Some transfer of control will be focused on teachers as well, for they are often the most knowledgeable members of the team in terms of developing appropriate classroom interventions. In a manner similar to that described above, teachers will be given increasing responsibility for developing interventions as treatment progresses. For the last two or three sessions, the therapist will provide feedback and guidance as the teachers attempt to develop school-based interventions on their own.

Homework Assignments

Most weeks, the child is given homework assignments consisting of speaking practice that is relevant for that child. These assignments proceed at a gradual pace, either according to the hierarchy constructed in advance (with input from child, parents, therapist, and teacher), or simply based on the child's progress following the initial assignment.

Homework assignment forms, both for in and out of school, are completed by the therapist for each assignment, and are sent home with the family each week to be returned the following week. Assignment forms for school-related tasks are written in a notebook or on forms that the parent transports to and from the teacher. All assignment forms should be reviewed with child and family the following week, and kept by the therapist for the duration of the treatment, but then given to the family to keep at the end of treatment. These materials can be helpful for review in the event that any symptoms recur in the future.

Appendix C includes copies of forms that can be photocopied as needed. We recommend that therapists make up three-ring binders with forms as appropriate. One of these binders could hold school-assignment forms to be passed between the parent and teacher. A second binder could hold homework assignments and other materials for the parents and child. A third binder might be kept by the therapist to retain completed assignment forms. Less formally, a simple spiral notebook can be passed back and forth among the therapist, parent, and teacher for communication.

With regard to forms, there are many forms included with the manual and it is not essential that all forms be used in order for the treatment to be effective. Treatment should be tailored to the needs of the child and family and that includes whether and which forms to utilize.

Chapter 2 *Pretreatment Assessment and Psychoeducation (Parent-Only Session)*

Materials Needed

- Selective Mutism Questionnaire

- School Speech Questionnaire

- Additional assessment measures as needed and obtained by therapist (e.g., Child Behavior Checklist, Eyberg Child Behavior Inventory, Social Anxiety Scale for Children, etc.)

- Copies of Treatment Letters (to Principal and Teacher)

- Educational handouts (optional)

- Weekly Homework Form

- Assignment binder or notebook

Outline

- Obtain and review detailed assessment of speaking behaviors

- Obtain further information regarding social anxiety symptoms if necessary

- Provide information regarding phenomenology of SM

- Provide information regarding cycle of avoidance

- Provide information regarding treatment program

- Assign homework

- Obtain information regarding speaking behavior from teacher

Assessment of Speaking Behaviors

Although at this point the child has probably already received the diagnosis of SM, detailed information regarding speaking should be obtained prior to beginning treatment—specifically, information regarding exactly to whom the child speaks, where he speaks, and in what situations. All of these variables will inform the treatment process, particularly the determination of a starting point for the treatment hierarchy. It is also valuable to know about the volume and other qualities of the child's voice. To gather some of this additional information, you can administer the Selective Mutism Questionnaire (see Appendix B) and review it with parents, and/or ask questions such as the following:

- To whom does your child speak comfortably and spontaneously?

- If your child does not speak to his current teacher, has he ever spoken to a teacher? If so, to which teachers and in what situations? Do teachers whom he speaks to seem to share certain characteristics?

- Does your child speak to any peers at school? All peers? Peers outside of school? In structured settings (e.g., dance, karate, sport teams) versus unstructured (e.g., playground, playdate)?

- Does your child speak to some friends only on the school yard but not when in class?

- Are there children that your child speaks to when he is not in school and then fail to speak to when he sees the same child at school?

- Does your child speak to you when in public (e.g., in stores) and nobody is paying attention to him?

- Does your child speak to strangers (e.g., answer questions such as, "How old are you?" or order his own food in restaurants)?

- When your child speaks reluctantly, how would you describe his voice (e.g., loud, soft, whisper)? Does he ever use an odd voice?

You will also want to obtain information regarding the parents' previous attempts to engage the child in speaking as well as how the child responded. Question the parents about the child's attitude about speaking, if they are aware of it (e.g., "Have you ever asked your child why he doesn't speak? What did he say?").

Assessment of Social Anxiety

Given that most children with SM also have non–speaking-related social anxiety, evaluation for the presence of social anxiety symptoms is warranted. Inquire as to whether the child appears anxious or is reluctant to engage in social activities that do not require speech, such as

- Blowing out candles at his own birthday party,

- Participating in new activities in a group (e.g., dance, bowling, sports),

- Participating in others' birthday parties (e.g., hitting the piñata),

- Participating nonverbally at school, or

- Simple nonverbal communication (nodding, pointing) when verbal communication is difficult.

Review with parents the impact of social anxiety versus SM on the child's current functioning (e.g., "Does anxiety in the nonspeaking situations that we have been talking about tend to cause significant problems for your child or keep him from doing things that he would like to do or should be doing?"). If the child has anxiety in both speaking and nonspeaking social situations, to achieve the best outcome treatment should aim at increasing comfort and participation in all social activities, regardless of whether speaking is involved.

Therapist Note

Children with SM often do not appear anxious when they are in situations where there is an expectation to speak. The explanation for this may be that the child with SM is so successfully avoiding verbal interaction that he no longer fully experiences the anxiety each time the situation occurs; he has simply discontinued all speech in the situations that produce anxiety. That is, as a result of a history of successful avoidance of speech, anxiety is no longer activated in these situations; the child is not feeling the pressure of anxiety about speaking, as they are no longer considering whether to respond. An analogy might be to imagine a person who is afraid of swimming. That person's fear is unlikely to be activated by sitting fully dressed in a chaise lounge by the pool. In contrast, if the swim-phobic person were in a bathing suit on the edge of the pool with his feet in the water, he would be quite anxious. This issue becomes important when the child's lack of anxiety in a situation when speaking is expected causes parents or others to falsely believe that his SM is not related to anxiety at all.

Phenomenology of Selective Mutism

First, ascertain parents' current attitudes and knowledge of the disorder. Correct any misperceptions about the causation and maintenance of the lack of verbal communication.

Common Misperceptions

Common misperceptions are often based on outdated information in the literature and may include these currently unsupported ideas regarding etiology:

- SM is related to disturbed family dynamics, especially as related to the mother–child relationship,

- SM is related to previous or ongoing trauma,

- SM is related to autism or other severe developmental disability, or

- SM is caused by a child simply refusing to speak to win a "power struggle."

Parental Guilt

Not surprisingly, parents may blame themselves for their child's failure to speak. Care should be taken to explain to parents that they are not the cause of the behavior, but that they can be instrumental in helping the child to overcome his problem. Parents may also feel guilt over their child's disorder based on their specific family circumstances ("Could this be related to my going back to work, our divorce, health, decision to have another child, etc.?"). It may be helpful to inform them that no consistent pattern of family circumstances, education decisions, birth order, and the like has been linked to the development of SM.

Nature of Selective Mutism

Next, present information regarding the nature of SM, being sure to include the information in the following script:

SM is commonly considered to be an anxiety disorder. The child's anxiety may be limited to speaking, or may be present in a variety of areas. Children with SM usually appear to be "shy" around other people, but shyness is not always a component of SM. Also, some children with SM do not even appear to be anxious, usually because they are so good at avoiding even attempts at speech.

Speech and Language Difficulties

Since speech and language difficulties occur more commonly among children with SM than among typically speaking children, briefly discuss this issue with parents. Unfortunately, there is little understanding of the nature of the speech and language problems among children with SM and exactly how these problems are related to the children's failure to speak. If parents are concerned about the presence of comorbid speech or language difficulties, or if you detect significant speech or language abnormalities, a referral to a speech and language pathologist (SLP) for evaluation is warranted. Evaluating the speech and/ or language of a child with SM is challenging, so parents should be advised to seek out an SLP who is familiar with SM. The American Speech-Language-Hearing Association (www.asha.org) can be a helpful source of referrals.

Also, if there is a severe articulation deficit (e.g., stuttering), verify that the child's speech is comprehensible before initiating behavioral therapy. This can be accomplished by obtaining from the parents a video recording of the child speaking, if feasible. Verifying that the child's speech is understandable first is important because if treatment proceeds without considering a significant articulation problem, a child may begin speaking and then be ridiculed by peers who cannot understand what the child is saying. Such a reaction could worsen the child's anxiety. In the case of a severe articulation problem, remediation of the articulation difficulty should precede treatment for SM. In the case of a severe language or communication disorder, it should be established that it is not the cause of the SM. In fact, a diagnosis of SM cannot be made in the absence of such a determination.

Nature of Avoidance

Discuss the reinforcing nature of avoidance. Explain to parents how children escape discomfort by not speaking in situations that are difficult for them (i.e., when speaking is successfully avoided, anxiety is reduced and avoidance is rewarded and reinforced). It is important that parents understand that avoidance is a primary part of the cycle of this disorder. The following script may be used:

> *When the child is allowed to avoid speech and the anxiety that comes with it, the lack of speech is "rewarded." In other words, selective mutism is reinforced when it allows the child to escape the unpleasant*

situation (speaking), making him more likely not to speak the next time around. This treatment will break this cycle by working with the child very gradually to speak, which usually means the child will get somewhat anxious at first, since they are no longer avoiding.

Overview of Treatment Program

Present the elements, structure, and goals of treatment to the parents as follows. Also, discuss the level of parent and teacher involvement required for successful treatment.

Elements of Treatment

Explain that there are three main elements of treatment and that each will be covered in further detail in future sessions.

1. **Graded exposure.** The child will gradually be exposed to situations requiring speech (in session, community, home, and school) with increasing expectation of child's successful production of speech. At first, children might not be actually speaking but taking small "steps" toward speech (e.g., mouthing words, making sounds, etc.).

2. **Contingency management.** A reward program that fosters systematic reinforcement of desired speaking behaviors (and efforts) will be developed and managed collaboratively by the therapist, parents, and teacher.

3. **Teamwork.** Parent, teacher, and child participation will be increased gradually as part of a team effort. Explain that at first you (the therapist) will clearly be the leader but will ask parents for their input. However, as time goes on, teacher, parents, and even the child will take more responsibility for the treatment. This is important because often work remains to be done even after formal treatment ends, and it is crucial that all involved are able to continue working after the therapist is no longer guiding them.

Structure

Describe the session structure, which typically follows this general sequence:

1. Parents, therapist, and child all review weekly assignments together.

2. Therapist and child complete exposure exercises. Presence of parent(s) will vary and is dependent upon child's speaking pattern and the requirements of each exercise.

3. For the last portion of the session, parents, therapist, and child all meet together to discuss new exposure assignments for the coming week. When possible, exposure assignments will follow from successful exposures that were accomplished in session with the therapist.

Goals

Present the general goals for treatment:

- Increased verbal communication,

- Increased social and academic functioning,

- Decreased avoidance, and

- Decreased distress associated with speaking.

Encourage realistic expectations in terms of the child's temperament and probable results of treatment (i.e., treatment is neither intended nor expected to turn a reserved child into an extrovert). Discuss this topic with parents further if necessary.

Parent Involvement

Explain to parents that this treatment requires their very active involvement, particularly as it relates to tasks that will be assigned for their child to complete between sessions. The tasks may involve interactions with extended family (e.g., grandparents, aunts, uncles), strangers, store clerks, and so forth. Some assignments may be time consuming or awkward for the parents (e.g., enduring periods of silence while their child is attempting to speak in a difficult situation, or introducing themselves to their child's peers' parents so that they can arrange playdates). Some assignments are planned to occur in the classroom under the teacher's supervision, but parents will still need to communicate the details of the assignments to the teacher and to take active responsibility to ensure that they occur. Although time will typically be allotted for discussion with parents during the session, if all parties agree, it can be quite helpful if one or both parents e-mail a weekly summary prior to each session to update the therapist prior to the session. If this additional communication occurs, it should not be hidden from the child. Due to constraints on therapist time, therapist may want to explain that even 1-way communication (from parent to therapist) where parent describes events of the week, is very helpful and that parent should not necessarily expect a reply from therapist.

Teacher Involvement

Explain to parents that because lack of speech at school is a major concerns increasing their child's speech at school will be a primary goal of treatment. As such, their child's main teacher will need to have significant involvement in the treatment program.

Therapist Note

Modify this section appropriately if the child is talking at school (highly unusual).

Although parent(s) will deliver a letter to the teacher that describes his/her role in the treatment, it is suggested that the therapist also speak to the teacher directly to introduce the treatment program and general process, and to find out how the child is functioning in the classroom. In addition, the parents will need to confirm the teacher's willingness to devote time and energy to the treatment program. The teacher's role will typically involve spending 5–10 minutes one or two times per week alone with the child, or with the child and selected peers. These meetings will need to occur before, during, or after school when no additional children are present. Parents can devise alternate systems for communicating with the teacher (e-mail, face-to-face communication) if both teacher and parents prefer, but written communication tends to be preferable. This guide provides an Exposure Assignment Form that can be photocopied; forms will be completed during the session and will contain instructions for the teacher. Parents will carry these forms back and forth between therapist and teacher. (Alternatively, a spiral notebook can be used to record assignments and can be passed among the therapist, parents, and teacher.) However, parents do not just function as passive means of transportation; they need to completely understand each school exposure assignment and be prepared to explain and/or clarify the instructions regarding the assignment to the teacher. Parents are also relied upon to check on the child's weekly progress at school (i.e., whether the teacher has attempted the assignment with the child). Although the teacher's collaboration and cooperation is vital, parents should not expect the teacher to take responsibility for the treatment.

Homework

All weekly assignments are recorded on the Weekly Homework Form found in Appendix C. See Figure 2.1 for a completed example. In addition, an Exposure Assignment Form for recording detailed instructions for both home and school exposures is provided in Appendix C and can be photocopied as needed. Standard homework for this session includes the following:

- Review educational material on SM (provide to parents as appropriate; see Appendix B for handout).

- Have parents provide Treatment Letters (see Appendix B) to the school's principal and the child's teacher as appropriate; these letters can also be used as the basis for a spoken conversation. Confirm teacher accessibility for treatment, and establish best way to communicate with the teacher (e.g., e-mail, phone). Encourage e-mail as it is usually the most effective.

- To obtain additional information regarding the child's speech at school, the School Speech Questionnaire (see Appendix B) can be given to parents to deliver to the teacher for completion. Given that the therapist will probably want to follow up with additional questions, it may be easier for therapist to administer the measure via telephone.

- Have parents bring in a binder in which to place school Exposure Assignment Forms that parents will deliver between therapist and teacher(s). As mentioned above, instead of using the assignment forms you may choose to use a notebook to record exposure assignments and then pass it back and forth among therapist, parent, and teacher.

WEEKLY HOMEWORK FORM

CHILD: ___Daniel___   THERAPIST: _____Natalie_____

THERAPIST CONTACT INFO: _____ _(297)_986-3431_____

DATE ASSIGNED: __2_ / _18_ / _12_   → SESSION NUMBER: ___1___

ASSIGNMENT DESCRIPTION

Assignment #1: _Daniel to tell Mom or Dad 1 thing (or his favorite thing) about today's_
session

Assignment #2: _Daniel to leave me a message telling me the same thing that he told his_
parent (about today's session).

Assignment #3: _Daniel to spend time in empty classroom at school with parent and a_
friend that Daniel speaks to or a sibling. Play "Go Fish" and "Hot and Cold".

Assignment #4: _Daniel and parent(s) to make list of rewards (small, medium, large) on_
the Prize Brainstorming Form and bring to next session.

Assignment #5: _Daniel to bring a favorite game from home to next session._

COMMENTS: _Daniel can decorate his assignment binder at home_

Please contact the therapist if you need any instructions of clarification.

Figure 2.1

Example of completed Weekly Homework Form

Chapter 3 | *Session 1: Introduction to Treatment and Rapport Building*

Materials Needed

- Props for rapport-building activities
- Prize Brainstorming Form
- Weekly Homework Form
- Exposure Assignment Form
- Assignment binder or notebook

Outline

- Welcome child to treatment
- Increase child's comfort speaking in therapy room (if necessary)
- Introduce goals/rationale for treatment
- Introduce use of reward program
- Begin to develop rapport with the child
- Assign homework

Welcome Child to Treatment

If this is your first time meeting the child (i.e., if you did not meet previously for an assessment visit), it is important to take some time to welcome the child by introducing yourself, showing the child around the setting, pointing out appealing toys, discussing the fun you will have in the room, and so forth. The child may or may not speak at this visit; the session content is such that it can be modified for either situation.

Child's Comfort in Therapy Room

Because places and people both affect inhibited behavior related to speaking, at the beginning of treatment it is important that the child feel comfortable speaking in the therapy room. It may be necessary to leave the child alone in the room with the parents to increase his comfort level. You may want to say something like the following:

> *I would like to have you and your parents spend some time in this room together so you feel okay being here. I would like you to get as used to the room as possible. A good way to show the room that you are comfortable is to be as loud as you can be and to make as much as noise as you want. I'll be back in a few minutes, so please show the room that you are really comfortable. I will knock to let you know before I come back in the room.*

Leave the parents and child alone in the room with toys or activities for 5–10 minutes. It is best if at least some of the toys or activities are ones that encourage loud or boisterous play. After that time period, knock, and reenter the room.

Goals and Rationale for Treatment

Discuss the child's knowledge about why he is in treatment. Because it is probable that the child will not be speaking to you at this point in treatment, questions will most likely be directed at parents and may include the following:

- Did you and [child's name] talk about why you were coming here? How did that conversation go?

- How did [child's name] seem to feel about coming here?

- Did [child's name] have any questions or concerns about what he would be doing here?

Introduce the goals and rationale for treatment to the child. As appropriate to the child's age, explain that the treatment will involve him practicing talking, and his parents and teachers will be helping him. You may wish to say something like the following:

*You may not know this, but there are other kids who also have a **hard time** talking in places such as school, even though talking at home is no big deal for them. I have worked with these kids and they say that they have more fun and things are easier for them when they talk everywhere, even at school. It can be hard work at first, but most kids are able to talk here after they get to know me [modify this statement if the child has no problems talking in therapy context]. I will work with you on talking here and talking at school, and your teacher and parents will help you too. We will work on doing things that may be a little bit hard at first, but you will help us decide what to work on to make sure that we don't pick something that is too hard for you.*

Therapist Note

"Hard time" is bolded in the preceding dialogue because the author strongly suggests using exactly those words. It is tempting to state that children are scared to talk, but many children don't describe their reluctance to speak as fear, so it is preferable to be more general and neutral by saying "hard time" rather than being more specific.

Reward Program

The reward program is an important part of the treatment. It may help motivate the child to speak, but more important, it will provide positive reinforcement for the effort that the child makes toward speaking. You may introduce the reward program as follows:

Because you may sometimes work hard on talking here or at school or other places, you will get fun rewards and prizes for working in this program. This is kind of like the way grownups get paid money for doing work at their jobs. At home this week, I'd like for you and your parents to think about and write down some things that might be good rewards for you—some small, some medium, and some big. Next week we will talk about them and decide which ones you might want to work for.

The size of prizes awarded will depend on how much work was done, over what period of time, and how difficult the work was. It is usually best for children to work for more frequent, smaller prizes rather than less frequent large ones. Examples of prizes include the following:

Small prizes: small toy (e.g., small stuffed animal, toy car, etc.), ice cream, an extra story at bedtime, a DVD rental, choice of family dinner.

Medium prizes: $10-$15 toy, trip to the movies, a special dinner out, sleepover with a friend.

Large prizes: amusement park, an arts and crafts party, a large toy.

Parents should help choose prizes and be comfortable withholding them if necessary. A form to help the family brainstorm about prizes is included in Appendix C. See Figure 3.1 for a completed example.

Building Rapport

To build rapport with the child, it can be helpful to engage in play activities with him. Conduct the following activities alone with the child (without parents present) except in extreme circumstances of separation anxiety. If the child can tolerate verbal communication with you, attempt to get to know the child by asking simple, forced choice or closed-ended questions about the child's family or, favorite activities during the play activities.

Therapist Note

While building rapport it is often easier to ask yes-or-no questions if the child is not speaking—it can be awkward to repeatedly ask open-ended questions that aren't answered. The child may answer yes-or-no questions simply by nodding or shaking his head. The goal of the activities at this point in the treatment is to build rapport, not necessarily to facilitate speech.

Small Prizes	Medium Prizes	Large Prizes
Favorite dinner	Whole day trip to the beach (lake, city, park, picnic etc.)	Amusement park
Baking for the afternoon	New book from the book store	EZ Bake Oven
Parent(s) play game(s) of choice for 45 minutes	Day or Evening out (dinner and movie)	Camping trip
Down load app on parent(s) phone	$15 Amazon Gift Card	iPod
Rent video	Sundae Bar at home	

Figure 3.1

Example of completed Prize Brainstorming Form

Suggested Play Activities

The following are suggested play activities; you may want to adapt or substitute depending on the age of the child.

- Blow bubbles (great fun if you can bring in a hair dryer and play "keep it up" with the bubbles).

- Decorate homework binder together.

- Various low-demand play activities: modeling clay, drawing, racing cars, puzzles, color wonder paints, glitter paint, finger painting, and so forth.

- Hide objects or pennies and give the child cues of "hot" and "cold" to indicate how close he is getting to the hidden objects. Switch roles and ask the child to hide the pennies for you and to give you the "hot" and "cold" cues. If this is too hard, he can use softer and louder clapping or other sounds to guide you. A recommended extension to this game is playing store at the end of the session and allowing the child to "buy" the prize he wants with the pennies that he has found. You can encourage the child to ask how much the desired prize costs if you sense that he might be able to do this with time and encouragement. Instead of suggesting that the child ask you "how much" a particular prize is, you can ask the child to count out pennies aloud to pay you with.

- Tell the child what objects are in a bag and take turns picking out particular objects with your eyes closed (if or when child is ready, do not tell him which objects are in the bag, and have him feel an object and name it aloud).

Homework

Discuss assignments with parents and child and write assignments down on the Weekly Homework Form (photocopy from Appendix C).

- Have the child tell parent one thing or his favorite thing that he did in session.

- Have the child leave you a phone message about which was his favorite thing, if he can tolerate doing this; otherwise, while in the child's presence, the parent(s) should leave you a phone message stating what the child reported was his favorite part of the session.

- Have the child speak while playing in an empty classroom with parent(s) (and a friend the child speaks to or sibling if possible). The specifics of what parent and child (and friend/sibling if they will be present) will be doing in the classroom should be decided during the session. The activity needs to be one that involves speaking.

- Have the child (with parents) make a list of rewards (small, medium, and large) on the Prize Brainstorming Form (see Appendix C).

- Have the child bring a game from home to play with in session.

- Have the child finish decorating his assignment binder or notebook (you can give the child stickers to take home).

Chapter 4 | *Session 2: Rapport Building, Reward System, Feelings Chart*

Materials Needed

- Completed Prize Brainstorming Chart

- Reward Chart

- Feelings Chart

- Situation Ratings Form

- Talking Ladder

- Playdate Form

- Classmate List

- Weekly Homework Form

- Assignment binder or notebook

Outline

- Review general events of past week, including any new speaking behaviors

- Review homework assignment and discuss noncompliance if necessary

- Develop reward system

- Introduce and practice using Feelings Chart

- Increase child's comfort speaking to parent(s) in therapy room if necessary

- Continue developing rapport

- Introduce Talking Ladder

- Begin discussing the child's interactions with peers

- Assign homework

Review of Past Week

Review events of the past week, including:
- Any significant environmental events;

- Selective mutism symptoms and their impact on functioning in home, academic, and social activities; and

- One positive thing the family or child did since last session.

Parents may do most of the talking during this review, but therapist comments should be addressed jointly to the parents and child, and the child should be included in discussion as appropriate. To include the child even if she is not speaking, make eye contact if the child can tolerate, direct some of your conversation and nonverbal gestures to her, and avoid speaking about her in the third person (as if she were not in the room). These strategies should be followed for most discussions with parents and child during the early part of treatment or any time the child is not verbally participating in discussion.

Review of Homework

Check on completion of assignments including the details of exactly what was done. Reward the child for any compliance with homework (e.g., stickers, verbal praise), and praise parents as well for their involvement. If the assignment was not done as assigned (e.g., child whispered instead of spoke), find out why and reassign.

In this and all future sessions, if the parents or child appear to be discouraged or embarrassed about homework that was not completed, be sure to frame the lack of completion as an obstacle and not as a personal failure. Then, either at this point or when assigning homework for the coming week, discuss how to remove barriers to accomplishing homework. Some common obstacles are failure to understand instructions regarding the assignment, not having enough time, lack of availability of teacher, and/or simply forgetting. If parents report that they did not attempt the assignment because they did not understand it, they should be encouraged to ask questions if they are unclear about the instructions for future assignments. It can also be helpful to ask them to restate (in their own words) their understanding of an assignment after you have explained it. If parents report that they forgot to do the assignment or had trouble finding time for it, work with them to establish a scheduled time during the week to complete the assignment. Working with teachers and their schedules is difficult, and parents (and therapists) need to be patient yet persistent in working with teachers to find time to complete assignments with the child. Assignments that were not completed should be done during the subsequent week.

If an assignment was not completed because it was "too hard," it should be modified (with input from child and parents) for next time. Parents and child should also be given feedback regarding the importance of alerting you in session if they realize that an assignment is likely to be too difficult.

Therapist Note

If parents appear to be unconcerned about not having completed an assignment, emphasize to them that out-of-session work is an essential component of this treatment program, and that it is unlikely that their child will benefit from the program if assignments are not consistently completed. This discussion is appropriate only after a few assignments have not been completed.

Development of Reward System

Review the rewards the family listed on the Prize Brainstorming Form for homework. Suggest adding other prizes if necessary. Focus on nonmaterial, small, and frequent rewards if possible. If the form contains only large, expensive items, work with the family to generate ideas for additional items so that child will be able to earn rewards sooner. You can explain that large prizes are earned after "lots and lots" of hard work is done.

Decide with the family how rewards will be earned. Discuss the importance of the reward system with the family and emphasize that the only rewards that should be given are the ones that are agreed in session were earned. In some cases, separate small rewards may be given in session to aid in building rapport, as well as to help create a positive association with the treatment setting and for reinforcing efforts made during the session. Here are possible ideas for earning rewards:

- Medium reward for a filled 10-sticker chart. Stickers are awarded at each session for completed weekly assignments (and stickers themselves may serve as small rewards).

- Larger reward for bigger chart (e.g., 20 stickers).

- Small rewards at each session (given by therapist) and an additional reward when chart is completed is an option if the child is very likely to need a great deal of reinforcement in session.

Discontinuing Other Reward Systems

Inquiry should be made as to whether parents are currently using any type of reward system in their home in attempts to affect other behaviors (school behavior, dressing, grooming, chores, getting along with siblings, etc.). If they are, you should suggest that they discontinue these systems so as to communicate that the focus now is working on speaking, and that is where the child is expected to put her effort. It is overwhelming and confusing for a young child to have more than one reward system going at a time. Prior to discontinuing any ongoing reward system, parents can choose to give the child a small reward so that she does not perceive the termination of that reward system as punitive. Later in treatment the parents and teacher will be asked to award prizes at their discretion.

Therapist Note

If the child enjoys such activities, you may choose to create and decorate a reward chart with the child. The following free charts are also recommended:

• Rocket Chart
(http://www.freeprintablebehaviorcharts.com/behavior%20 charts%20single%20pdf/Rocket%20Chart%20Line.pdf)

• Flower Chart
(http://www.freeprintablebehaviorcharts.com/behavior%20 charts%20single%20pdf/Flower%20Chart%20Line.pdf)

Feelings Chart

See Figure 4.1 for the Feelings Chart; a copy in Appendix C has also been provided to photocopy for the homework binder. Possible language to use for introducing the Feelings Chart might be as follows:

We will use the Feelings Chart to help us talk about different things that happen and how you feel about them. The pictures show how you feel about something; either how happy or good you feel or how bad or scared you feel about it. The numbers get higher when you are feeling more uncomfortable, just like your temperature gets higher when you are sick and have a fever. When the red is higher on the picture of the feeling thermometer, it means feeling worse. There are also faces to go along with the thermometers and numbers. The less happy faces are to show when you feel less happy or more upset or scared about something. The hands are to show how much bad or upset feelings there are or how hard something is. Hands a tiny bit apart is not any bad feelings, but as the hands get more far apart it is to show more bad or upset or scared feelings. So, if I ask you how hard is it or how bad do you feel when you are eating ice cream, what would you say?

We may use the Feelings Chart to rate how easy or hard it is to talk at different times.

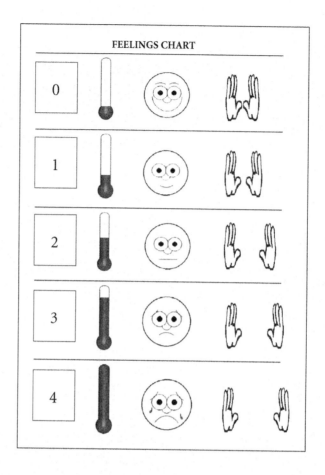

Figure 4.1

Feelings Chart

Take some time in session to practice using the Feelings Chart. Also, encourage parents to practice using it at home a few times (consider adding this to the formal homework assignment). Note that the youngest or least advanced children are likely to have trouble using any rating system or may use it in idiosyncratic or inaccurate ways. If this is the case, you may discontinue use, or just adapt to the way individual child tends to use the feelings ratings. Also, younger children tend to have the easiest time with "hand" ratings.

Therapist Note

> *As with the reward chart, with your or parent's help, a motivated child can create her own feelings chart in place of the one provided.*

Child Comfort in Therapy Room

As in Session 1, it may be necessary to increase the child's comfort speaking in the therapy room. If needed, have the child spend time talking to parents alone in the therapy room (without your presence). This can help promote the child's use of verbal communication in your office. Before you exit, inform the child that you are going to knock and reenter the room in 5 minutes and then do so.

Development of Rapport

Continue developing rapport with the child. Do activities together that have no verbal requirement (modeling clay, toy cars, drawing, building blocks, puppets, video games, etc.). If the child brought game from home, play the game.

As in Session 1, conduct these activities alone with the child (without parents present) except in extreme circumstances of separation anxiety. If separation anxiety continues to be a problem, parents can remain in the room, but give parents paperwork to complete and ask that they sit in a corner of the room to complete it. Prior to the next session, speak to the parents about standing up and leaving to make a phone call during the next session if the child continues to protest being alone with you.

Introduction of Talking Ladder

Introduce the Talking Ladder (see Figure 4.2 for a completed example). This is a hierarchy of situations that the child will be working on during therapy. Explain that situations at the bottom of the ladder will be easier, situations in the middle of the ladder will be of medium difficulty, and the situations at the top will be the hardest. To prepare for creating the hierarchy, the family will make a list of easy, medium, and hard situations for homework; some of these situations will involve speaking but will be less specific than those on the Talking Ladder. You may want to begin this list in session. A Situation Rating Form is provided in Appendix C to assist in making this list (see Figure 4.3 for a completed example).

Instructions: List situations to work on, with the easiest situations at the bottom of the ladder and the hardest situations at the top.

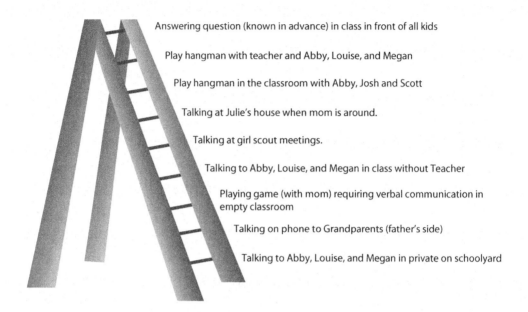

Answering question (known in advance) in class in front of all kids

Play hangman with teacher and Abby, Louise, and Megan

Play hangman in the classroom with Abby, Josh and Scott

Talking at Julie's house when mom is around.

Talking at girl scout meetings.

Talking to Abby, Louise, and Megan in class without Teacher

Playing game (with mom) requiring verbal communication in empty classroom

Talking on phone to Grandparents (father's side)

Talking to Abby, Louise, and Megan in private on schoolyard

Figure 4.2

Example of completed Talking Ladder

Talking With Peers

Children with SM often have problems speaking with their peers. The treatment process will focus a fair amount on increasing speech to peers. Therefore, parents will initially need to provide information regarding their child's peers and the child's comfort speaking to these other children. Confirm that the parents know or can obtain the names of their child's classroom peers. If this presents a problem help parents problem-solve (e.g., discuss with teacher or school administration). The focus on increased communication with peers will involve speaking with peers at school, but also (and often initially) will involve the child working on speaking to peers in her own home; thus, this will involve the parent repeatedly inviting children over for playdates as often as possible. For children who are not having difficulty speaking with peers at school, much of this section will not be included in treatment.

SITUATION RATING FORM

Instructions: Describe specific situations and how difficult they are. Some of these situations should NOT include speaking and should be very easy situations so that this task is not overwhelming. Others should be speaking situations.

EASY:

Situation: _____Getting dressed in morning_____

Situation: _____Talking to parents_____

Situation: _____

MEDIUM:

Situation: _____Whispering to mom's best friends_____

Situation: _____

Situation: _____

HARD: (Rating 8–10)

Situation: _____Talking in the playyard at school_____

Situation: _____Talking to teacher_____

Situation: _____Talking in voice to mom's best friends_____

Figure 4.3

Example of completed Situation Rating Form

Therapist Note

For therapists who are working with more than one child with SM, combining sessions so that the children can practice together can be a wonderful opportunity. Even if one of the children has generalized social phobia, this can still work out.

Playdates

Homework for this week will include a playdate with a student in class whom the child does not currently speak to regularly, but rates as "easy" to try to speak to. If the child seems unable to give a rating, have parents make this determination from what they know or have them ask the teacher with which peers the child seems most comfortable (e.g., when playing). If the child is not yet talking to peers, parents may attempt to have her speak to them (parents) in front of her playmate (e.g., parents ask child nonthreatening forced-choice questions such as, "Would you like apple juice or milk for snack?"). Ask parents to be prepared to report on the child's behavior (including whether the child used any verbal communication) during the playdate and to use the Playdate Form (see Appendix C) to record these observations. Discuss the parents' role in facilitating play but suggest that parents briefly observe whether both children become spontaneously engaged in play. If they don't, parents should be prepared to step in and create a fun and engaging play situation (e.g., baking, creating homemade "gak" or Play-Doh, building with blocks or LEGOs, and putting together puzzles). Videogames and TV are to be avoided. Unstructured, imaginative play is also unlikely to be successful if children are having difficulty engaging and playing together. Counsel that, if necessary, the parent can join children in play, but should remain on the sidelines as much as possible and exit the play when children seem engaged with each other. In general, the playmate's parent(s) should be strongly discouraged from being directly involved in the playdate (although at this young age it is very likely that one or both of the playmate's parents will have stayed during the playdate with their child).

Homework

Discuss assignments with parents and child and write assignments down on the Weekly Homework Form (photocopy from Appendix C).

- Have child and parents together write down a list of situations (ideally, at least some involving speaking and some not—e.g., jumping rope) with ratings of easy, medium, and hard on a Situation Rating Form (see Appendix C to photocopy). You will review these situations with the parent and child at the next session and use them as the basis for building the Talking Ladder.

- Have parent bring in list of students in the child's class (see Classmate List form in Appendix C).

- Assign "at home" playdate with student in class to whom the child does not regularly speak but rates as "easy" to play with or to try to speak to. Emphasis should not be on speaking during this early assignment. Communicate to parents that they should observe the majority or significant portion of the playdate so that they are able to report on their child's behavior (both verbal and nonverbal). A Playdate Form is provided in Appendix C.

Chapter 5   *Session 3: Class Chart, Talking Ladder, Exposure Practice*

Materials Needed

- Completed Situation Ratings Form

- Talking Ladder

- Feelings Chart

- Completed Classmate List

- Class Chart

- Other Individuals List

- Playdate Form

- Weekly Homework Form

- Exposure Assignment Form

- Assignment binder or notebook

Outline

- Review general events of past week, including any new speaking behaviors

- Review homework and discuss noncompliance if necessary

- Develop chart using list of peers

- Discuss and construct Talking Ladder (hierarchy) using the completed Situation Rating Form and Feelings Chart

- Practice exposure in session

- Discuss exposure exercises

- Plan for out-of-session exposure

- Assign homework

Review of Past Week

Review events of the past week, including:

- Any significant environmental events;

- SM symptoms and their impact on functioning in home, academic, and social activities (i.e., did anything come up in the last week that was a problem caused by SM?); and

- One positive thing the family or child did since last session.

Parents may still do most of the talking during this review, but the child should be encouraged to participate using the strategy described in Session 2.

Review of Homework

Check on completion of assignments and discuss, in particular, what parents observed during their child's playdate. Reward any compliance with homework (e.g., with stickers or other prizes recorded on the child's Reward Chart). Reframe noncompliance to encourage family members and discuss how to remove barriers to accomplishing assignments over the coming week (see session 2 for particular problem-solving strategies for noncompliance).

Therapist Note

If exposure exercises reveal that a particular game or type of play is successful at eliciting the child's speech, further engagement in this

*activity should be restricted to when the child is attempting to speak
in difficult situations. This is done to ensure that the child doesn't
tire of or get bored with the particular activity. This idea may need
to be repeated more than once to parents. Emphasize that even if the
child clearly wants to play the game again during typical play, he or
she should be kept from doing so; this action can have the additional
benefit of increasing the reward value of the game itself.*

Talking With Peers

Take the list of students in the child's class that was completed for
homework and turn it into a chart that includes details about the child's
verbal interactions with these classroom peers (see Figure 5.1). Possible
variables to incorporate include the following:

- amount of speech (e.g., none, one word, normal spontaneous
  speech),

- where child speaks (e.g., in class, playground, outside of school), and

- how the child speaks (only in a whisper, normal voice, odd
  voice).

A column to indicate whether the child has had a playdate with each
classmate and whether the child has spoken to the classmate's parent(s)
can also be helpful. Use pictures, stickers, or markers to decorate the
chart and make it fun. Fill in the chart to reflect the child's current
level of communication and activity with peers; keep a photocopy of the
baseline chart for comparison at treatment termination.

Development of Talking Ladder

You will begin to develop the Talking Ladder in this session using the
completed Situation Ratings Form. First, however, review the purpose
of using the Talking Ladder.

CLASS CHART

Child's Name	Description of Speech	Where Speech Has Ocurred	Quality of Speech	Playdate?	Spoken To Child's Parents?
Daniel	Yes/No response to questions— 1 x only	Playground	Soft voice	No	No
Marcy	Normal spontaneous speech— regularly	Playground and classroom	Regular voice	Yes	No

Figure 5.1

Example rows of completed Class Chart

Purpose of Talking Ladder

Explain the concept behind the Talking Ladder in further detail. This explanation could go something like this:

> *If you remember, last session I explained that we were going to be making a Talking Ladder. Talking situations that are easiest but that you still need to work on will go on the bottom steps and those will be the ones that we do first. Everyone has their own ladder with different steps. I gave you homework to think of what situations we should put on the steps on the ladder for you. We will work on the steps on the bottom of the ladder first, because just like a real ladder, you get can't get to the top without starting at the bottom and climbing up. It is good to start at the bottom of the Talking Ladder where the situations are easier for you because you will get better and better at talking as you move up to harder situations.*

You may want to explain the use of the Talking Ladder by using a metaphor of getting into a cold pool:

> *Some people think of this as kind of like getting into a pool slowly by putting a toe in first to get used to the water, and then slowly getting in*

with the rest of your body. With the Talking Ladder, you take a step at a time and wait until you get used to talking before taking the next step.

Ordering Situations

The "easy situations" on the list that don't involve talking will not go on the Talking Ladder but can be discussed briefly to contrast the difference between the easy and more difficult situations. If there are no appropriate, relatively easy talking situations on the list because they are either all too easy or all too difficult, work with the family to develop appropriate tasks. At the upper end of the Talking Ladder, there is no need to include the most difficult tasks from the Situation Rating Form—in fact, it is often best to intentionally exclude these from the ladder because at this stage the child is likely to be frightened and/or overwhelmed by the notion of attempting very difficult tasks. Early in treatment, the function of the Talking Ladder is to establish a starting place for exposure exercises. As the child progresses it will be updated, and the more advanced tasks can be added then.

Because you will be working with the parents and child to develop exposure assignments that correspond to items on the ladder, items must be detailed enough to allow for initial development of assignments. If the list presented wasn't specific enough (e.g., listed "talking at school" instead of talking to teachers vs. peers or in classroom vs. playground), work with them to make at least some initial items more specific.

Help the child use the Feelings Chart to rate some situations listed on the Talking Ladder (if the child is capable). If the child has trouble, you or the parents may assist with this task by asking the child to indicate (e.g., with hands apart) how easy the talking situations at the very bottom of chart and very top of chart would be for him. You can also ask the child to rate two adjacent situations relative to each other ("Which is easier, this or this?"), and then rearrange their order if necessary.

Therapist Note

Beginning this session, and throughout the rest of treatment, when possible, you should use language that focuses on which tasks on the Talking Ladder are "easier" than others rather than which are "harder." This is because you want to help the child develop an attitude that considers how to alter scary situations so that they are easier instead of focusing on the difficulty of tasks. Focusing on the difficulty of tasks higher on the hierarchy can cause the child to get overwhelmed by negative emotion and fear and make it more difficult to engender a spirit of motivation and desire to change.

In-Session Exposure

In-session behavioral exposures provide an excellent opportunity to identify interventions that are most likely to be successful for a particular child across settings and individuals. For the typical child who finds it difficult to speak to a new adult (the clinician) in session, it is likely that several different exposure interventions will be attempted as the desired behavior (speech) is gradually shaped. Use of the successful exposure tasks in other settings is an important strategy in achieving generalization of therapy gains. For most children, these first in-session exposures will involve speech to or in front of you and should proceed naturalistically, without discussion that they are exposures or assignments. Therefore, Feelings Chart ratings are usually not recommended for these initial in-session exposures with the therapist.

General Tips

Here are some general tips for in-session exposures:

1. **Periods of Silence:** Always allow plenty of time for the child to respond to you. In typical interpersonal interactions, silence can be awkward and most people avoid it and use chatter to fill in silences. When working with a child with SM, periods of silence are important and often necessary to give the child time to respond.

2. **Revising Exercises:** If the child does not respond after a significant amount of time, assume that the exercise was too difficult and revise the same exercise to make it easier.

3. **Oppositionality:** If the child seems to be declining participation in an exercise due to oppositionality (though this can be difficult to discriminate from reluctance due to anxiety), switch to a different

exercise rather than changing the current one. Also, consider an immediate, positive reinforcer for engaging in the exercise. To avoid a power struggle over the child's participation in any given exercise, allow for short breaks for easy, relaxed activities such as drawing or puzzles before getting back to work. Inform the child that after successful "work," a longer period of fun or play will follow. If the child declines participation in any activity that you suggest (such as drawing, puzzles, blocks, etc.) this may be an indication that oppositionality and not anxiety is the underlying influence. Increasing the attractiveness of the activity should be considered. For example, offering a craft activity (modeling clay, finger painting, beads, glitter glue) a more active activity (racing toy cars), or desirable game may help circumvent the development of a detrimental cycle.

4. **Presence of parents:** Some children with SM find it harder to speak in difficult situations in the presence of parents, whereas others find it easier if their parents are there. Parents may initially believe that they are aware of the child's preference (i.e., which is easier), but they are often incorrect. In most cases, children are more likely to speak to a new person when not in the presence of their parents. Therefore, unless parents strongly believe that the opposite is true, when in-session exposures are focused on speaking directly to a new person (and not just in front of a new person), these attempts should be undertaken without parents present. Later, when the child is comfortable speaking to the new people or in new situations, including the parents can be the next step.

Therapist Note

For some children, you will want to consider using in-session rewards to reinforce (and possibly motivate) speaking exposures with you. This is typically more important with younger children who are reward oriented and have more difficulty understanding the future benefits of the treatment. In addition, receiving rewards in session will increase the likelihood that the child has a positive association with treatment. Toward this end, it can be beneficial to give the child a small reward following the first session regardless of whether he has engaged in exposure exercises. If you choose to use in-session rewards, these should be small, token rewards (e.g., stickers, tattoos, small toys), and should not replace the rewards that parents will provide.

Choosing Initial In-Session Exposures

Depending on the severity of the symptoms and the course of the sessions thus far, the child may or may not be speaking to you or in front of you at this point. If he is doing neither, the initial in-session exposures will most typically center on exercises aimed at eliciting the child's speech in your presence. With a child who has extreme social anxiety that goes beyond reluctance to speak, early exposure exercises may need to focus on eliciting nonverbal responses (see Chapter 13 for discussion of treatment of general social anxiety). The following is a suggestion for an in-session exposure exercise aimed at eliciting speech in the presence of the therapist. See Appendix A for additional ideas for in-session exposure exercises.

Integration Into Game

1. Child begins to play a game with his parent while the therapist sits in the farthest corner of the office and clearly ignores the game (types on computer, reads, listens to voicemail messages). After about 5 minutes, begin adding a short comment or two (nothing that requires a response) about the game that they are playing to indicate that you were aware of their activity after all. In between comments, you should go back to ignoring their game.

2. Depending on the child's reactions to your comments (ignoring, freezing, smiling, etc.), shorten your physical or emotional distance by varying amounts. Some choices are: moving your chair closer; staying where you are but increasing your focus on the game between parents and child; increasing the number of comments you make, including interactive comments with parents; moving to sit near parents and child and watch the game; and various combinations of these.

3. Continue decreasing your emotional/physical distance slowly as much as the child can tolerate, up to and including joining the game. One recommended approach is to join so that the child and parent(s) are playing as a "team" with the child communicating (even in a whisper) to his parent. Then, at some point, indicate that you can hear the child (e.g., respond directly or comment). In this way, the child will gradually begin to realize that you are hearing his voice, and anxiety over the issue will dissipate. Refrain from directly asking the child open-ended questions at this point unless making the clinical judgment that the child is ready for this task. Integration into a game may take place over more than one session. Each time the integration is attempted anew, it is likely that you will need to return to an earlier step.

Discussion of Behavioral Exposures

Further explanation of the idea of behavioral exposures should be given at this time, whether or not exposures are begun in session. Explain that, beginning with an easy thing on the Talking Ladder, the child is going to do some talking challenges to learn that they are really not so hard after all. If the child has already done exposures, review them, discussing how the child will continue with similar challenges, and giving the child positive reinforcement. This discussion could go as follows:

I know that you have already tried some new talking to people that you don't usually talk to [or "talking in places that you are usually silent," if that is more appropriate] *and that was probably a challenge. That's great that you already got started working. This is the kind of thing that we are going to be working on here.*

If the child has done exposures suggested by parents that were too difficult (and did not go well), discuss these as follows:

I know that there were a couple of times recently when you tried to speak in new situations (or to new people) and this seemed too hard or too scary. Maybe this was higher up on the ladder than you were ready for.

When this happens, hard exposures should be discontinued and tried again later. Or, hard tasks can be altered so that they are less difficult. Consider discussing how this is done using the example of the failed exposure attempt (work with the family to come up with modifications to change the difficulty of the specific exposure that they attempted).

Out-of-Session Exposure Tasks

Each exposure to be completed for homework should be recorded on its own Exposure Assignment Form. See Figure 5.2 for a completed example. A blank copy is provided in Appendix C for photocopying. Retaining copies of the filled-out forms is advised.

As this is the first time that you are assigning an out-of-session exposure task, explicitly discuss the importance of the graduated approach and working together to assign exposure tasks. Explain that jumping ahead and asking a child to speak in situations that are further up on the Talking Ladder can interfere in the treatment process—*especially at the beginning*. Specifically, trying hard situations too soon and failing may reinforce the child's negative feelings about speaking and the discomfort associated with it. The reverse is not true; that is, modifying an exposure exercise to make it easier if the child is unable to complete the exposure as assigned is acceptable and is a commonplace occurrence. It is important that the child experiences success early on to build confidence. In addition, a successful completed experience demonstrates to the child that "nothing bad" happens when he speaks to someone new or speaks in a new situation. Additionally, as should be emphasized to the teacher, particularly at this early phase of treatment, it is important to construct exposure situations exactly as assigned. This is important because even relatively minor changes can alter the difficulty of the assignment. For example, the child may be able to tolerate speaking to a particular child but not another, so changing the peer involved in the assignment could drastically affect the difficulty. Similarly, changing location, others who are present, and content of speech can all change the difficulty of the assignment for the child.

EXPOSURE ASSIGNMENT FORM

CHILD: __Gracie_____ PARENTS: __LISA, BILL_____

EXPOSURE WITH (CIRCLE ONE)
   (TEACHER) Ms. Grinblatt PARENT: _____ OTHER: _____

DATE ASSIGNED: _3_ / _1_ / _12_   → SESSION NUMBER: _3_____

ASSIGNMENT DESCRIPTION

a) Assignment: __Read first paragraph of Wemberly Worried (book) to mom in classroom while Ms. Granite sits at her desk doing paperwork (ignores Gracie and mom)__

b) Reward expected: _____Sticker on chart_____

* *

PARENT/TEACHER, PLEASE RECORD OUTCOME: ● COMPLETED
                                          ○ NOT COMPLETED

Please Describe Outcome of Assignment

It was difficult to hear Gracie because she whispered very quietly.

Therapist Notes on Assignment

c) Outcome of assignment: ○ Not attempted–not possible
                                 ○ Not attempted–child did not tolerate
                                 ○ Attempted not completed
                                 ● Completed as assigned
                                 ○ Completed with modification

                Child's feeling rating after exposure: 😊 😐 😮 😕 😣

                Check here _____ if child rating not obtained

Explain outcome: _Gracie read in whisper (barely audible)._

Figure 5.2

Example of completed Exposure Assignment Form

Modeling From In-Session Exposures

When possible, out-of-session exposure exercises should be modeled after successful in-session exposure exercises. In particular, exercises that were successful with the therapist should be considered for their application with the child's teacher. For example, a child who plays a game with their parents while the therapist does not pay attention (see preceding example) could be assigned to do the same task with the teacher. Although the tasks assigned will often be related to the task that was targeted during the session, the setting and other participants will obviously be different, and these variables should be carefully considered and incorporated as per the child's Talking Ladder. The assignments should be reviewed in detail so that each family member knows exactly what the exercise entails (e.g., where it is to take place, who is to be present, where they are to stand, how long it is to last, etc.).

Rewards

A reward value should be assigned to each exposure and other assignments. Record the reward to be given on the Exposure Assignment Form. Furthermore, care should be taken to ensure that each family member is in agreement as to the exact nature of the reward to be earned and what needs to be done to earn it. In most cases, the determination of whether the reward was earned by the child is one that will be made by the therapist and not by the parent; this is to limit conflict between the parent and child in cases where there is ambiguity.

School Assignments

A school-based task, if assigned, is discussed in detail and agreed upon in session. Allow ample time for questions and clarifications so that child and parent both understand the plan for the school assignment. If the teacher is involved, as will usually be the case, the nature of the assignment will be communicated to him or her in writing using an Exposure Assignment Form (to be delivered by a parent as discussed in Chapter 2).

Homework

Discuss assignments with parents and child and write assignments down on the Weekly Homework Form (photocopy from Appendix C).

- Have the child complete exposure tasks as decided in session.

- Have the parents deliver school assignments to the teacher if appropriate.

- Have the child repeat a playdate with the same peer as last week (if the playdate went relatively well) or choose another child if it did not (if it was nonverbal AND noninteractive). Parents should allow children to spend time playing somewhat independently at first. Then, parents should attempt to observe whether their child is using any verbal communication by coordinating play activities that involve speech (see Appendix A) and, if necessary, getting involved in play themselves. The presence of the peer's parent is likely to increase anxiety related to speaking and, for this reason, it is strongly recommended that the peer's parent should not be present in the play area.

- Ask the family to create a list of individuals outside of school for future work. The list may include both children (from sports, church, Scouts, etc.) and adults (extended family, parents' friends, doctors, etc.). Forms (Other Individuals List, Other Individuals Chart) are provided in Appendix C.

Chapter 6   *Sessions 4–9: Intial Exposure Sessions*

Materials Needed

- Talking Ladder

- Feelings Chart

- Copies of returned Exposure Assignment Forms or other information regarding outcome of school and other assignments

- Class Chart and/or Other Individuals Chart

- Playdate Form

- Weekly Homework Form

- Exposure Assignment Form

- Assignment binder or notebook

Outline

- Review general events of past week

- Review homework and discuss noncompliance if necessary

- Develop, explain, and execute in-session behavioral exposures according to individual plan

- Devise and discuss relevant out-of-session activities

- Assign homework

Review of Past Week

Review events of the past week, including:

- Any significant environmental events;

- SM symptoms and their impact on functioning in home, academic, and social activities;

- Changes in speech patterns (i.e., words to new people or in new places, or not speaking in situations or to people previously speaking); and

- One positive occurrence since the last session.

At this point in the treatment, the child may be more actively participating in this discussion, particularly the last element (describing a positive occurrence).

Review of Homework

Review assignments. Praise all efforts and discuss attempts to problem-solve any logistic difficulties (probably parent related) and fear-related difficulties. Ask child to rate how difficult exposures were, regardless of whether they were completed. Exposure assignments that were too difficult should be altered so that they are easier and can be tried again the following week.

If necessary, problem-solve barriers to compliance with the parents and/ or child. This may need to done at an alternate time and/or location if there is not enough time in session.

Therapist Note

During this period of checking in, or at other times, parents may express frustration with their child's lack of speech. Model appropriate praise for child's efforts and remind them that improvement is incremental and proceeds according to a graduated hierarchy. It is likely that the situations in which the parents are eager to see their child speak are still too difficult. You can explain that success with the current exercises will lead to progress speaking in other areas as well.

In this way, the parent will understand the relevance of early work that might otherwise appear to be unimportant. You may consider reviewing some of the analogies used initially when presenting the graduated approach to treatment (e.g., getting into a cold pool).

In-Session Behavioral Exposures

Develop, explain, and execute in-session behavioral exposures according to individual plan and course of treatment. Again, exposures may or may not include parents, other individuals, and you. The family may even be asked to bring in individuals for exposures (extended family, child's peer, etc.). The addition of a sibling may be helpful, not as an exposure per se, but to add some fun if the child is not responding positively to exposures. Exposures may occur in or out of the therapy room, and may involve a wide variety of activities as discussed in Session 3 (see Appendix A for suggested exposures).

Development of Exposures

Exposures should be individually developed based upon the child's symptom profile and previously successful exposure exercises. For example, if a child successfully spoke to the parents while playing a particular game or activity while you were in the room but were not paying attention, the next exposure should repeat the same task with your increased involvement rather than starting a different task in which you will become more involved. With regard to individualizing, there are children with SM who would have no difficulty speaking to a therapist even upon first meeting. When working with such a child it clearly would not make sense to focus on tasks with goals of elicitation of speech with you.

Use the Feeling Chart to have the child provide input as you work together to develop exposure exercises in session. See the following example:

You said it would be too hard to play "Go Fish" with your mother and me together. Can you point to where you would rate that on the Feelings Chart? What if your mother came in and sat over there while you and I played. How would you rate that? What if she sat there but turned her back to us?

The child does not need to verbally communicate ratings but can hold up fingers, point, or do other things to communicate.

Pre- and Postexposure Ratings

If the child is able to accurately use the Feelings Chart, she can use ratings before attempting an exposure. Preexposure ratings provide a gauge of the child's anticipatory anxiety and may help guide and confirm that you are not pushing the child too far. Obtaining a rating following successful completion of an exposure is then also recommended. Postexposure ratings are usually considerably lower than the anticipatory rating and are therefore useful for later pointing out to a child that "it wasn't as hard as you thought it would be." In this way, the child can begin to understand that they may be overestimating the negative outcomes related to speaking. This understanding can serve as the foundation for the cognitive component of the treatment if the particular child is developmentally advanced enough to use additional cognitive strategies for combating anxiety. Another related concept is to refer back to the last exposure and discuss whether anything bad happened. If the child is able to reflect on the absence of a negative outcome resulting from the last speaking event, it is likely to decrease their anxiety regarding the next one.

It is not uncommon for children to think that just about any speaking exposure will be too challenging and to therefore rate all exposures as "4." If this happens despite attempts to modify the exposure being discussed, it should be assumed that the child does not understand the use of the Feelings Chart, and its use should be discontinued. Alternately, if the child rates all exposures as too difficult, the therapist should consider suggesting two presumedly easy exposures ideas and letting the child choose which one to try.

Out-of-Session Exposure Tasks

Based on the success of the in-session task, upcoming events in the child's life, and the child's Talking Ladder, devise out-of-session tasks (school, home, and community) and assign their reward value. Ideally, the child and parents will be involved in devising the assignment. Elicit their ideas regarding assignments by saying something like the following:

Although I will be giving you the ideas and framework for the out-of-session assignments, you know more about what is going on in your lives than I do and your ideas are very helpful for developing good assignments. Can you tell me about what you guys will be doing in the next week that may provide some good opportunities for practice?

Discuss all exposure assignments and record each on an Exposure Assignment Form (photocopy from Appendix C). Retaining copies of the filled-out forms is advised.

Involving the Teacher

Assignments that involve the child's teacher should be written on school Exposure Assignment Forms to be given to the teacher by the parents (e.g., in a binder). To confirm and give the teacher an opportunity to request clarification or ask questions, the assignment can also be verbally described to the teacher in person by the parents, by telephone by you, or via e-mail. However, given that there are usually several short assignments involving the teacher, it will probably not be possible to speak to the teacher about each one.

Homework

Discuss assignments with parents and child and write assignments down on the Weekly Homework Form (photocopy from Appendix C).

- Have the child complete exposure tasks as decided in session.

- Have the parents deliver school assignments to teacher.

- Have the parents schedule playdate(s) as decided in session.

Chapter 7 | *Session 10: Treatment Midpoint Session*

Materials Needed

- Talking Ladder

- Feelings Chart

- Copies of returned Exposure Assignment Forms or other information regarding outcome of school and other assignments

- Class Chart and/or Other Individuals Chart

- Playdate Form

- Weekly Homework Form

- Exposure Assignment Form

- Assignment binder or notebook

Outline

- Review general events of past week

- Review homework

- Review progress to date

- Problem-solve obstacles to progress

- Devise and discuss relevant out-of-session activities

- Assign homework

Review of Past Week

Review events of the past week, including:

- Any significant environmental events;

- SM symptoms and their impact on functioning in home, academic, and social activities;

- Changes in speech patterns (i.e., words to new people or in new places, or not speaking in situations or to people previously speaking); and

- One positive occurrence since the last session.

At this point in the treatment, the child may be more actively participating in this discussion, particularly the last element (describing a positive occurrence).

Review of Homework

Review assignments. Praise all efforts and discuss attempts to problem-solve any logistic difficulties (probably parent related) and fear-related difficulties. Exposure assignments that were too difficult should be altered so that they are easier and they can be tried again the following week.

Review of Progress to Date

Using copies of completed assignment forms or other materials that will allow you to review the child's treatment status, discuss any progress that is evident. You may begin the conversation by saying something like the following:

Here we have copies of the assignment forms from all the things that you have tried and your class chart. I also have your Talking Ladder. Let's look at all of these things together and see if we can figure out if speaking has gotten any easier in any of these situations or if it is easier to speak to any people that it was difficult to speak to before.

If the child is receptive, you could make this a competition to see who can name the most new or improved speaking behaviors. This activity can be done alone with the child (if the child is speaking freely with the therapist), and then the information can be shared with the parents and their input solicited, or it can done together with the parents and child. Progress may include speaking to more people, the same people but in more situations or settings, speaking more loudly or with more expression, or speaking to more people at once.

To obtain information about progress at school, this week's homework will include sending a note requesting teacher feedback regarding any noted changes in the child's speaking behavior.

Revision of Talking Ladder

If significant progress has occurred with regard to speaking behaviors, create a revised Talking Ladder in consultation with the child and parents. This may include more difficult situations that were previously excluded, or may simply involve repositioning situations that have become easier with practice. This can be a good opportunity to remark on positive changes in the child's speaking behaviors and to praise the child for improvement.

Problem Solving of Obstacles

If little progress is detected, work with the parents and child to determine the cause for the lack of treatment success. Following are some possible causes.

Teacher noncompliance with exposure tasks: If the teacher has been unable to attempt tasks with the child for 75% or more of the assignments, this is a likely interference in treatment. Consult Chapter 13 (Additional Treatment Considerations) for additional strategies.

Child noncompliance or willfulness: A child's repeated resistance to attempting tasks, even when the parents and therapist agree to modify difficulty. Similarly, child's comments that he is not going to talk no matter what should be interpreted as a factor that is likely to affect success in treatment. Consult Chapter 13 (Additional Treatment Considerations) for additional strategies.

Parent noncompliance with reward system: Parents have been giving extra rewards or not following through on rewards that were earned. Meet privately with parents to obtain details about the problems following the reward system. Explain the importance of the planned reward system with regard to the treatment program (it might be helpful to refer back to the initial explanation of the reward system in Chapter 3). Sometimes it may be necessary for the therapist to take over administering the reward program, including keeping possession of the rewards (if they are material objects). In most cases, problems with families following the reward system require the therapist to work more closely with the family on this aspect of the treatment.

Lack of generalization of exposure: The child successfully completed assignments as assigned, but in later identical situations that arose spontaneously, the child repeatedly failed to speak. In general, after a child has successfully accomplished a speaking task at least two times in different but similar situations, she should be assigned to "always" respond verbally in that situation. If the child has trouble doing this, additional assignments including variation in key elements can be focused on. Then a second attempt should be made at having the child respond verbally every time they are in the situation. If the lack of generalization occurs with a specific person (i.e., the child only speaks to a given person when fulfilling an assignment), this may be remedied by increasing the number of assignments, by varying the contexts in which the assignments occur, or by varying the nature of the speech within the assignments. Spontaneous speech, in particular, is most difficult and is not likely to occur if not practiced specifically.

Parental noncompliance with exposure tasks: Parents repeatedly "forget" to try tasks with the child or otherwise fail to present opportunities for the child to attempt exposure assignments. The importance of the exposure tasks should have been made clear to parents prior to beginning treatment, with frequent reminders when necessary. The analogy of learning to play an instrument is an apt one; a child cannot learn to play piano if he doesn't play except when at the lesson. If there is another family member or close friend who can take over this aspect of the treatment, this may be a solution. If this is not an option, and if the parent(s) repeatedly fail to arrange for exposure assignments, you may need to suggest that treatment be terminated for the present time. Alternately, medication treatment, which typically requires less time investment, may be an option, and a referral for a medication evaluation with a qualified child psychiatrist can be offered.

Consult Chapter 13 (Additional Treatment Considerations) for additional strategies for overcoming some of these obstacles to treatment response.

Out-of-Session Exposure Tasks

As in previous sessions, consider upcoming events in the child's life and the child's Talking Ladder to devise out-of-session tasks (school, home, and/or community) and assign their reward value. Ideally, the child and parents will be involved in devising the assignment. Elicit their ideas regarding assignments by asking about possible opportunities to practice during upcoming events.

Discuss all exposure assignments and record each on an Exposure Assignment Form (photocopy from Appendix C). Retaining copies of the filled-out forms is advised.

Involving the Teacher

Assignments that involve the child's teacher should be written in school Exposure Assignment Forms to be given to the teacher by the parents (e.g., in a binder). If there have been chronic problems with teacher noncompliance, and you have not recently communicated with teacher, a brief communication at this point is recommended to facilitate compliance.

Homework

Discuss assignments with parents and child and write assignments down on the Weekly Homework Form (photocopy from Appendix C).

- Have the child complete exposure tasks as decided in session.

- Have the parents deliver school assignments to teacher along with a note requesting teacher feedback regarding any noted changes in the child's speaking behavior.

- Have the parents schedule playdate(s) as decided in session.

Chapter 8   *Sessions 11–14: Intermediate Exposure Sessions*

Materials Needed

- Talking Ladder

- Feelings Chart

- Copies of returned Exposure Assignment Forms or other information regarding outcome of school and other assignments

- Class Chart and/or Other Individuals Chart

- Playdate Form

- Weekly Homework Form

- Exposure Assignment Form

- Assignment binder or notebook

Outline

- Review general events of past week

- Review homework and discuss noncompliance if necessary

- Develop, explain, and execute in-session behavioral exposures according to individual plan

- Devise and discuss relevant out-of-session activities

- Assign homework

Review of Past Week

Review events of the past week, including:

- Any significant environmental events;

- SM symptoms and their impact on functioning in home, academic, and social activities;

- Changes in speech patterns (i.e., words to new people or in new places, or not speaking in situations or to people previously speaking); and

- One positive occurrence since the last session.

At this point in the treatment, the child may be more actively participating in this discussion, particularly the last element (describing a positive occurrence).

Review of Homework

Review assignments. Praise all efforts and discuss attempts to problem-solve any logistic and/or fear-related difficulties. Exposure assignments that were too difficult should be altered so that they are easier and they can be tried again the following week.

If necessary, problem-solve barriers to compliance with the parents and/or child. This may need to done at an alternate time and/or location if there is not enough time in session.

In-Session Behavioral Exposures

Develop, explain, and execute in-session behavioral exposures according to individual plan and course of treatment. Again, exposures may or may not include parents, other individuals, and you. The family may even be asked to bring in individuals for exposures (extended family, child's peer, etc.). Exposures may occur in or out of the therapy room, and may involve a wide variety of activities as discussed in Session 3 (see Appendix A). As in earlier sessions, the addition of a sibling or friend that the child speaks comfortably with may be helpful, not as an exposure, but to help add positivity, if the child tends to have a negative attitude toward exposures in session.

Development of Exposures

Exposures should be individually developed based upon the child's symptom profile and previously successful exposure exercises. For example, if a child has recently had success responding to your questions with one-word answers (e.g., answers "What is your favorite color?"), at this session the focus could be on child speaking a whole sentence (e.g., asking the therapist, "What is your favorite color?").

Pre- and Postexposure Ratings

As in previous sessions, if the child has mastered use of the Feelings Chart, she can use ratings before attempting an exposure, as well as upon completing the exposure. Pre-exposure ratings provide a gauge of the child's anticipatory anxiety and ensure that you are not pushing the child too far. Obtaining a rating following completion or attempt of an exposure can be helpful, as ratings are usually considerably lower than the anticipatory rating and are therefore useful for later pointing out to a child that "it wasn't as hard as you thought it would be." In this way, the child can begin to understand how speaking becomes easier after practice. These ratings do not need to be recorded on a form, just noted for future reference tasks.

Out-of-Session Exposure Tasks

Based on the success of the in-session task, upcoming events in the child's life, and the child's Talking Ladder, devise out-of-session (school, home, and/or community) tasks and assign their reward value. Ideally, the child and parents will be involved in devising the assignment. Elicit their ideas regarding assignments by asking about possible opportunities to practice during upcoming events.

Discuss all exposure assignments and record each on an Exposure Assignment Form (photocopy from Appendix C). Retaining copies of the filled out forms is advised.

Involving the Teacher

Assignments that involve the child's teacher should be written in school Exposure Assignment Forms to be given to the teacher by the parents (e.g., in a binder). Remind parents that they should make every effort to pass the assignment binder or notebook to the teacher at a time when there may be a minute to discuss assignments or general issues surrounding the treatment.

Homework

Discuss assignments with parents and child and write assignments down on the Weekly Homework Form (photocopy from Appendix C).

- Have the child complete exposure tasks as decided in session.

- Have the parents deliver school assignments to teacher.

- Have the parents schedule playdate(s) as decided in session.

Chapter 9 — *Session 15: Continued Exposure and Introduction of Transfer of Control*

Materials Needed

- Talking Ladder
- Feelings Chart
- Copies of returned Exposure Assignment Forms or other information regarding outcome of school and other assignments
- Class Chart and/or Other Individuals Chart
- Playdate Form
- Weekly Homework Form
- Exposure Assignment Form
- Assignment binder or notebook

Outline

- Review general events of past week
- Review homework and discuss noncompliance if necessary
- Develop, explain, and execute in-session behavioral exposures according to individual plan
- Devise and discuss relevant out-of-session activities for child
- Begin transfer of control process with explanation of concept
- Assign homework

Review of Past Week

Review events of the past week, including:

- Any significant environmental events;

- SM symptoms and their impact on functioning in home, academic, and social activities;

- Changes in speech patterns (i.e., words to new people or in new places, or not speaking in situations or to people to whom he was previously speaking); and

- One positive occurrence since the last session.

Remember to involve the child in this discussion as much as possible, particularly when reviewing the last item (positive occurrence).

Review of Homework

Review assignments. Praise all attempts and discuss any logistic difficulties (probably parent related) and fear-related difficulties. At this point in the treatment, if there are chronic issues with assignments not getting done, it is important to evaluate whether the child is getting sufficient opportunity to practice. If there has been little or no evidence of improvement to this point, and the family has routinely failed to complete assignments, the parents should be made aware that there is little chance of any improvement without a significant change in this pattern. Help them realistically evaluate whether it is possible to continue the program given the time commitment that is required for a positive result.

In-Session Behavioral Exposures

At this point in treatment, it is likely that the child is speaking to you, and in-session exposures are probably not geared toward eliciting single words. However, full, spontaneous speech with you may not have been achieved and could be a worthy goal. In addition, if there are stores or doormen, security personnel, or other new people nearby, they could provide opportunities for in-session exposures that focus on other individuals who are unknown to the child. In some cases, there may be very little to practice in session if all remaining difficulties center on school. If this is the case, much of the session time may be spent reviewing and preparing for out-of-session exposure tasks. Alternately, therapist and child can role-play or "practice" particularly difficult speech-related interactions. For example, many children with SM have difficulty responding with "please," "thank you," their name, and verbal greetings. Interventions for these activities are described in Appendix A: Suggested Exposure Exercises.

Transfer of Control and Out-of-Session Exposure Tasks

Parents should be present for review of in-session tasks and current status of the child's exposure hierarchy (i.e., what is still left to address on the Talking Ladder). Explain to the family in practical terms the theoretical basis for transfer of responsibility and control—that often when treatment ends there are still more challenges to work on, and therefore they need to be capable of continuing to work on their own. Remaining sessions will be a chance for the family to practice planning these assignments with you still here to help them. Proceed as follows:

- Elicit parents' and child's ideas for out-of-session tasks.

- Provide feedback to shape appropriate exposure exercises as needed.

- When agreement as to out-of session exposure exercises is reached, collaboratively assign reward values.

Record each exposure on an Exposure Assignment Form (photocopy from Appendix C). Retaining copies of the filled out forms is advised.

Discuss assignments with parents and child and write assignments down on the Weekly Homework Form (photocopy from Appendix C).

- Have the child complete exposure tasks as decided in session.

- Have the parents deliver school assignments to teacher.

Chapter 10 *Sessions 16–17: Continued Exposure With Additional Focus on Transfer of Control*

Materials Needed

- Exposure Ideas Form
- Talking Ladder
- Feelings Chart
- Copies of returned Exposure Assignment Forms or other information regarding outcome of school and other assignments
- Class Chart and/or Other Individuals Chart
- Playdate Form
- Weekly Homework Form
- Exposure Assignment Form
- Assignment binder or notebook
- Discretionary sticker (for parents' use)

Outline

- Review general events of past week, including any new speaking behaviors
- Review homework and discuss noncompliance if necessary
- Develop, explain, and execute in-session behavioral exposures according to individual plan

- Facilitate transfer of control while shaping out-of-session plans for behavioral exposures for the coming week

- Assign homework

- Assign parents to award "discretionary sticker."

Review of Past Week

Review events of the past week, including:

- Any significant environmental events;

- SM symptoms and their impact on functioning in home, academic, and social activities;

- Changes in speech patterns (i.e., words to new people or in new places, or not speaking in situations or to people previously speaking); and

- One positive occurrence since the last session (have child describe).

Review of Homework

As part of the transfer of control practice, parents (and in some cases, the child) should have had much more involvement in planning and assignment of specific exposure exercises. The review of homework should reflect this increased responsibility and include critical discussion of what might have gone better. Relatively more time should be spent on this review than in previous weeks. Questions to ask might include:

- How did everything go with homework this week?

- What did you think of what we picked to do? Was it too easy? Too hard?

- What could you have done to change it to make it easier/harder?

In-Session Behavioral Exposures

As in the previous session, in-session exposures may be relatively less central to the session at this point in treatment. If areas of difficulty remain that are amenable to in-session work, exposures should be done, but typically more time will be spent on review and planning of out-of-session exposures.

Out-of-Session Exposure Tasks

Parents again should join for much if not all of the discussion of the current status of the child's exposure hierarchy (i.e., what is still left to work on the Talking Ladder). Reiterate that they will continue to work together after treatment ends and that remaining sessions will be a chance for the family to practice planning these assignments with you still here to help them. Proceed as follows:

- Elicit parents' and child's ideas for out-of-session tasks.

- Provide feedback to shape appropriate exposure exercises as needed.

- When agreement as to out-of session exposure exercises is reached, collaboratively assign reward values.

Record each on an Exposure Assignment Form (photocopy from Appendix C). Retaining copies of the filled out forms is advised.

Involving the Teacher

In addition to exposures that the therapist/parents assign, the teacher will be asked to generate (in writing) specific ideas for school-based exposure exercises for the following week. This request may be communicated via email or by phone, or, if necessary, the teacher can be provided with a form where they can provide their ideas for exposures (see Figure 10.1; a blank Exposure Ideas Form is included in Appendix C). If they are not able to provide specific ideas for exposures, they will be asked to provide information regarding the areas in which the child is still having difficulty speaking.

Exposure Ideas Form

CHILD: _Emily_ PARENTS: _Lisa, Bill_ TEACHER: _Ms. Grinblatt_

DATE ASSIGNED: _5 / 3 / 12_ → SESSION NUMBER: _16_

(Therapist to complete above)

- -

General Areas of Remaining Difficulty

Speaking to me in front of other children.

Specific Ideas for Exposures

Play Animal Guessing Game or Interview Game during recess with me (teacher)

and increasing number of peers (best friend Michelle first)

Figure 10.1

Example of completed Exposure Ideas Form

Transfer of Control Sticker Exercise

To continue facilitating transfer of control, in addition to the usual exposure assignments, give parents a "discretionary sticker" to award to the
child during the week for prompted speaking behaviors. Discuss what
sorts of speaking behaviors are appropriate for parents to encourage and
reward with this sticker. If necessary, shape the discussion to emphasize
tasks that are similar to those that the child has already accomplished
but are just slightly more difficult. Get suggestions from parents as to
what they think might be good ideas for this exercise and provide appropriate feedback. Note that these stickers will be given for behaviors that
are undertaken separately from assigned exposure tasks. Often, the best
behaviors for this assignment are ones that are likely to occur naturalistically during the upcoming week. For that reason, query as to what
the family has planned to help them problem-solve opportunities that

might present themselves for speech challenges. Parents should complete an Exposure Assignment Form for the speaking behavior that they prompted.

Homework

Discuss assignments with parents and child and write assignments down on the Weekly Homework Form (photocopy from Appendix C).

- Have the child complete exposure tasks as decided in session.

- Have the parents prompt speaking behavior, award discretionary sticker, and complete Exposure Assignment Form on their own for this speaking behavior.

- Have the parents deliver school assignments to teacher.

- Have the parents deliver Exposure Ideas Form for elicitation of teacher's school assignment ideas (if therapist is not going to get these directly).

Chapter 11 *Sessions 18–19: Continued Exposure and Transfer of Control/Review of Progress*

Materials Needed

- Talking Ladder

- Feelings Chart

- Copies of returned Exposure Assignment Forms or other information regarding outcome of school and other assignments

- Class Chart and/or Other Individuals Chart

- Playdate Form

- Weekly Homework Form

- Exposure Assignment Form

- Assignment binder or notebook

- Discretionary sticker (for parents' use)

Outline

- Review general events of past week, including any new speaking behaviors

- Review homework and discuss noncompliance if necessary

- Develop, explain, and execute in-session behavioral exposures according to individual plan

- Review progress and remaining goals for treatment

- Continue facilitation of transfer of control and planning behavioral exposures for coming week

- Address transfer of control as it pertains to the child

- Assign homework

Review of Past Week

Review events of the past week, including:

- Any significant environmental events;

- SM symptoms and their impact on functioning in home, academic, and social activities;

- Changes in speech patterns (i.e., words to new people or in new places, or not speaking in situations or to people previously speaking); and

- One positive occurrence since the last session (have child describe).

Review of Homework

As part of the transfer of control practice, parents (and in some cases, the child) should have had much more involvement in planning and assignment of specific exposure exercises. The review of homework should reflect this increased responsibility and include critical discussion of the exposure process. In addition, relatively more time should be spent on exposure assignment review than in previous weeks. Questions to ask might include:

- How did everything go with homework this week?

- What did you think of what we picked to do? Were some too easy? Too hard?

- What could you have done to change them to make them easier/harder?

- Did you [your child] get a sticker? What was it for? If no, was a sticker offered?

In-Session Behavioral Exposures

Develop, explain, and execute in-session behavioral exposures according to individual plan. At this point in treatment there may be little to work on in the treatment setting. As mentioned previously, relatively more time may be spent reviewing out-of-session exposures and planning for future out-of-session exposures.

Review of Progress

Note and reinforce positive changes the child has made during treatment in terms of symptom reduction and increased family, school, and social functioning.

Pinpoint areas in which difficulties remain. Identification of current interference and distress caused by symptoms of SM will help guide the construction of new exposure tasks.

Transfer of Control and Out-of-Session Exposure Tasks

As in Sessions 15–17, facilitate transfer of control while shaping plans for behavioral exposures for the coming week.

1. Elicit parents' and child's ideas for out-of-session tasks. Guide them in using upcoming events when possible to develop tasks.

2. Provide feedback to help shape appropriate exposures exercises.

3. When agreement on out-of session exposure exercises is reached, collaboratively assign reward values.

Record each exposure on an Exposure Assignment Form (photocopy from Appendix C). Retaining copies of the filled out forms is advised.

Similar to what was done in the previous few sessions, give parents a discretionary sticker, but this time it will be up to the child to decide on something for her to do during the week to earn the extra sticker. If there is time, have a short discussion to elicit ideas from the child. Parents can be involved in the award of the discretionary sticker by suggesting activities that might be worthy of a sticker as opportunities arise, or by reminding the child about the sticker, but they should not push. This reward is for the child to practice self-rewarding if doing so is motivating for her.

Involving the Teacher

Outside of session (via phone call), provide teachers with feedback on their ideas for exposures and give suggestions for ideas for ongoing exercises to work on. If it is difficult to reach teachers on the phone, consider e-mail, or sending an informal note.

Homework

Discuss assignments with parents and child and write assignments down on the Weekly Homework Form (photocopy from Appendix C).

- Have the child complete exposure tasks as decided in session.

- Instruct the parents to hold the discretionary sticker for the child to use.

Chapter 12 *Session 20: Relapse Prevention and Graduation*

Materials Needed

- Copies of returned Exposure Assignment Forms or other information regarding outcome of school and other assignments

- Progress Chart

- Remaining Goals Worksheet

- Certificate of Achievement

- Assignment binder or notebook

Outline

- Review general events of past week, including any new speaking behaviors

- Review homework and discuss difficulties

- Review progress and present graphic representation of improvement (could be child's own chart or something that you constructed)

- Continue discussion of remaining goals

- Discuss future speaking challenges and relapse prevention

- Have graduation fun, including presentation of diploma

Review of Past Week

Review events of the past week, including:

- Any significant environmental events;

- SM symptoms and their impact on functioning in home, academic, and social activities;

- Changes in speech patterns (i.e., words to new people or in new places, or not speaking in situations or to people previously speaking); and

- One positive occurrence since the last session (have child describe).

Review of Homework

Due to the transfer of control practice, parents (and in some cases, the child) should have had much more involvement in planning and assignment of specific exposure exercises. The review of homework should reflect this increased responsibility and include critical discussion of what might have gone better. Questions to ask might include:

- How did everything go with homework this week?

- What did you think of what you picked to do? Were some too easy? Too hard? Did you try making changes to make them easier/harder?

- Did you give yourself a sticker? What was it for? Did you feel really proud of yourself for doing that? Could you have imagined doing that a few months ago?

Review of Progress

Lead a discussion of the progress the child has made by focusing on how much things have changed since you first met the child. Include a review of specific speaking behaviors that the child regularly engages in

---

PROGRESS CHART: <u>ASHLEY'S</u> ACCOMPLISHMENTS!

Instructions: Use the space below to record the child's progress, for example, categories might include classmates, other kids, teachers, family members, or other adults.

With classmates at school:
- Playing talking games (e.g., Sam, Laura)
- Asking questions as part of interview games (e.g., Jack, Ava)
- Speaking to other children during small group activities led by Mrs. Meyer and Mrs. Green
- Having lots of fun playdates outside of school (e.g., Julia, Marcy)

With other kids:
- Offering stickers to kids at ballet
- Answering questions from kids at church
- Having lots of fun playdates (e.g., Wendy, Katie)
- Playing games and talking to friends' siblings

With teachers:
- Playing talking games (Mrs. Meyer, Mrs. Green, Ms. Fern)
- Asking and answering questions, including yes/no and factual questions
- Talking about pictures, drawings, toys, and daily activities
- Leaving messages
- Saying "hi" and "thank you"

With family members:
- Answering questions (e.g., aunts, uncles)
- Asking questions as part of "race" games (e.g., grandpa, James, Chelsea)
- Leaving short and long messages (e.g., dad, aunts, uncles)
- Practicing reading lists (e.g., mom, grandpa)

With other adults:
- Ordering for self and family at stores and restaurants
- Leaving short and long messages (e.g., Ms. Deanna, Ms. Ashley, Sister Luymes)
- Talking on the phone (e.g., Trina, Katharina)
- Saying "thank you" at stores, doctor's office, and UCLA
- Talking about pictures and drawings (e.g., art teacher, Lindsey, Lu)
- Asking questions to friends' parents (e.g., Jacob's mom, Sophie's mom)

Figure 12.1

Example of completed Progress Chart

that were previously either very difficult for the child or were completely avoided. Remember that because these behaviors are now easy and more routine, the child (and the family) may have forgotten that they are actually huge accomplishments. Also, because treatment tends to progress in small steps, it is easy for those involved to "miss" the progress taking place. Parents and teachers should be reminded to reward the child with praise and positive comments. Similarly, it is beneficial for the child to acknowledge his own efforts and success.

To facilitate recognition of the child's accomplishments, a Progress Chart listing the changes in the child's verbal communication with

REMAINING GOALS WORKSHEET

GOAL	EXPOSURES	REWARD
Talking to boys in class	1) Play story book game with teacher and 1 boy present (add more boys over time)	Sticker on Chart
	2) Ask each boy favorite color (see exposure examples)	Sticker on Chart

Figure 12.2

Example row of completed Remaining Goals Worksheet

others should be constructed and reviewed with the family (see Figure 12.1 for a completed example). This chart is generated by reviewing the child's assignments sheets, Talking Ladder, filled-in Class Chart, and Other Individuals Chart. If time allows, the child can participate in constructing the Progress Chart. In some cases, progress may not be overwhelming in magnitude. Nevertheless, even when slight, the child's progress should be acknowledged.

Remaining Goals

Using previous discussions and the initial exposure hierarchy or Talking Ladder as guides, identify several remaining goals for continued focus. Record these goals onto the Remaining Goals Worksheet (see Figure 12.2 for a completed example). In addition, devise potential exposure exercises that might be helpful in attempting these goals and also record these on the Remaining Goals Worksheet. Last, discuss possible rewards for reaching goals and record these as well. Leave some blank spaces on the worksheet for additional goals that might be identified by the family at a later date.

Future Speaking Challenges and Relapse Prevention

Although relapse is rare with SM, returning to school after long absences or vacations may be difficult for a child. If significant symptoms recur, parents should consider using interventions similar to those used during treatment.

If a child does begin to show signs of reluctance to speak, parents should refer to the completed assignment sheets (ideally kept in a binder) for interventions. Encourage parents to feel free to return to treatment or consult with you as needed.

Tips for Relapse Prevention

Give parents the following tips for relapse prevention:

- Be watchful for even minor avoidance of speaking and take care not to "fill in" for the child's speech.

- Occasionally provide rewards for speech that appears difficult for the child, and acknowledge the child's continued efforts in overcoming anxiety with speaking.

- If there are situations that may be challenging, head off failure by modifying situations so that the difficulty faced by the child is more gradual.. For example, arrange for the child to meet his new schoolteacher privately in advance of the start of the school year.

Graduation Fun

At the end of treatment, be sure to set aside some time for celebration. Participate in a fun activity with the child, such as playing a game, going for ice cream, and engaging in some other activity of the child's choice.

Present the child with a certificate of achievement and positively reinforce the family for their effort and participation in treatment. A blank certificate for your use is provided in Appendix C. You may photocopy and distribute or use it as a model for creating your own.

Chapter 13 *Additional Treatment Considerations*

Working With Teachers

Research has shown that the vast majority of children with SM have significant difficulty speaking at school, and their teacher is the person with whom speaking tends to be most difficult. Therefore, it is likely that the child you are working with is probably not speaking very much at school, and is either having difficulty speaking to the teacher in general, or is having difficulty speaking to the teacher if other children are nearby. When this is the case, it is vitally important to get the classroom teacher involved as an active participant in the child's treatment and this treatment manual is designed to achieve such a goal. Making initial contact with the teacher may be easily done by sending a letter and then following up with a phone call. A sample Treatment Letter to the teacher is included in Appendix B. Unfortunately, teachers may be disinclined to devote time to participating in treatment because they fail to perceive the child's lack of speech as problematic, do not understand the nature of SM, or face perceived or actual time constraints.

Failure to Perceive the Problem

In contrast to children with more externalizing problems, a child with selective mutism is unlikely to cause disruption in a classroom and may not come to the attention of the teacher. Thus, the teacher may not realize that the child's lack of speech is adversely affecting the child's ability to learn and achieve in the classroom. Of course, if the child is not asking questions, requesting clarification, or expressing confusion when necessary, the learning process is certainly affected. Importantly, social and emotional development are also primary goals of the early elementary years, and a child not speaking to peers will lag in these areas as well.

Misunderstanding of SM

The second issue in working with teachers, misunderstanding the nature of SM, refers to the some teachers' tendency to perceive a child's reluctance to speak as a willful refusal rather than as an anxious avoidance behavior. If a teacher perceives the child's behavior as an obstinate behavioral choice, he or she is understandably more likely to get frustrated with the child and less likely to put forth a patient effort toward collaboration with the treatment team. One of the easiest and most successful ways to correct misunderstandings regarding the nature of SM is to provide education about the disorder. This can be done by simply referring teachers to websites, encouraging parents to loan teachers books, or supplying teachers with photocopies of review articles such as those cited in the reference section of this manual. A brief overview of SM is also included as a handout in Appendix B.

Enhancing teachers and administrator's understanding of the disorder is a priority in that it helps get buy-in to the treatment as they learn that they can be important and central figures in the resolution of the problem. As the therapist, you can bring additional classroom relevance to the treatment by emphasizing the ways in which the child's additional verbal communication can help the teacher evaluate academic skills and learning processes. Toward this end, in discussing the specifics of school-related treatment goals, a focus on those obviously linked to the teacher's objectives is most likely to help build an alliance with the teacher and clarify the relevance of the treatment to the classroom.

Perceived or Actual Time Constraints

Given that the teacher's participation in the treatment requires extra time outside of the classroom, it is prudent to minimize the time requested. Toward that end, always be very clear and specific regarding the intervention and make every attempt to keep exercises limited to a few minutes. Generous appreciation of the teacher's time should be expressed often, and suitable gratitude should be modeled for parents as well. If the teacher's instincts regarding exposures and intervention in general are appropriate and comparable to your treatment plan, time can be saved by allowing the teacher to devise his or her own exercises with the child (assuming that communication remains clear and direct between all parties).

It is not uncommon for a teacher to miss an exposure assignment over the course of a week or two. In fact, this is more the rule than the exception. However, when a teacher is either chronically unavailable for exposures, forgets them, or even tells you outright that he or she cannot participate in treatment, proceeding as usual with this program would not make sense. Before giving up on the teacher, steps should be made to problem-solve any difficulties, especially if you and the teacher have not spoken personally up to this point. Perhaps exposure exercises can be done during classroom time, or the parent can take on more of the responsibility for the school exposures. If it does not work for the teacher to be involved in the treatment, it may be possible to find a different staff or faculty member at school who is in close contact with the child and is both interested in and able to participate. This could be, for example, a reading specialist, school psychologist, or speech teacher.

Adaptations for Older Children

Although SM treatment is most often sought for young children, older children do sometimes continue to suffer from the disorder. If an older child does present for treatment, care should be taken to confirm that SM is the primary concern and that there are no comorbidities present that would cause behavioral therapy to be an inappropriate treatment approach.

This manual is based on a treatment developed for children up to 8 years, and as such, includes limited emphasis on cognitive techniques that are typically a component of CBT for anxiety-based disorders.

Therefore, when treating a child older than 8 years who has typical cognitive functioning, one likely would want to supplement the treatment with additional material typically found in traditional CBT for anxiety. For example, older children (8 years and over), who are usually capable of more abstract thinking than younger children, are likely to benefit from the addition of treatment components such as relaxation (e.g., see Koeppen, 1974; Ollendick & Cerny, 1981), breathing exercises, mindfulness (see *Still Quiet Place: Mindfulness for Young Children* by Amy Saltzman, MD, http://www.cdbaby.com/cd/amysaltzmanmd3), and imaginal exposure exercises that will vary depending on the feared situations.

Comorbidity

It is not uncommon for children with SM to have comorbid conditions, and these would have likely been detected during a pre-treatment diagnostic evaluation. Two of particular relevance are social anxiety and oppositionality.

Social Anxiety

As mentioned previously, clinical levels of distress over speaking around other people is usually a symptom of social anxiety, and the majority of children with SM meet additional criteria for social anxiety as well. Therefore, children receiving this treatment will likely have symptoms of social anxiety that go beyond discomfort with speech or verbal communication. Luckily, during this treatment process, the fear habituation tends to generalize beyond speaking situations, thus providing relief for non–speaking-related social anxiety as well. Among children with severe SM and comorbid social anxiety, it may be more effective to initially address the nonspeaking elements of social anxiety within the hierarchy (e.g., giving high fives, initiating movements, following commands), as these are often less fear inducing. If a child presents for treatment with primary social anxiety disorder and secondary SM—that is, the lack of speech causes less interference as the general social anxiety—this treatment program may not be the most suitable one. A broader social anxiety treatment approach should be considered instead.

Oppositionality

As discussed in Chapter 1, there are conflicting data regarding whether children with SM display increased rates of oppositional behavior. In the past there were many who believed that oppositionality was part of the etiology of the disorder, and there is a history of SM having been incorrectly attributed to defiance or willfulness. While it is possible that an individual child's lack of speech is not primarily due to anxiety, but instead due to an effort to assert control, be defiant express anger, and so forth, this is not usually the case. To determine whether the child's lack of speech is due to anxiety or not, it can be helpful to observe the child's behavior for signs of anxiety; if anxiety around speaking is absent, other motivations for lack of speech are more likely. It is essential to remember that this treatment is closely based on treatment for anxiety, and follows the assumption that the lack of speech is primarily related to anxiety. If that is not the case, it follows that this treatment is not likely to be effective. The primary treatment recommendation for refusal to speak for other reasons is parenting work with a qualified specialist.

Psychotropic Medication

When very little or no progress is made after 12 sessions or so, the possibility of referral to a qualified child psychiatrist for a medication evaluation should be considered. The addition of a psychotropic medication, usually an SSRI, may be recommended. These have been shown to be effective at targeting anxiety symptoms that have an impact on speaking (The Research Unit on Pediatric Psychopharmacology Anxiety Study Group, 2001). Many parents are understandably reluctant to put young children on psychiatric medications, but the child's functioning, development, and quality of life need to be considered. When and if a decision is reached to begin medication, some parents struggle with how to discuss psychotropic medication use with a young child. Some children are frightened when told that medicine will make it easier for them to talk (thinking that the medicine would cause them to speak even if they didn't want to). In general, most mental health professionals do not suggest administering medication to children without their knowledge. The decision of what to tell a child regarding their psychiatric medication can be discussed in detail with the child psychiatrist. Although SSRIs are clearly effective in reducing social anxiety among children, continuing with behavioral therapy can further benefit the child through the experience of overcoming an obstacle by establishing and meeting behavioral goals.

Appendix A: Suggested Exposure Exercises

The majority of these are clinic-based exposures to be replicated at school (with teachers and/or peers) or at home with other individuals.

Initial Exercises to Facilitate Speech to Therapist While Speaking to Parent

- Talk to parents (in context of playing game or reading) in empty therapy room with door closed.

- Talk to parents in therapy room with door closed but with therapist right outside.

- Talk to parents in therapy room with therapist outside and door slightly ajar with hands over ears and eyes closed.

- Talk to parents in therapy room with therapist outside and door increasingly more ajar with hands over ears and eyes closed.

- Talk to parents in therapy room with therapist outside and door open and hands over ears/eyes open.

- Whisper to parents in front of therapist.

- Play board or card game with therapist by whispering to parents; therapist responds to child's whispers without parent repeating child's words to therapist (i.e., therapist needs to "overhear" the whisper).

PURCHASED GAMES THAT ARE HELPFUL

- I Have Card Game (University Games)
- The Storybook Game (Fundex Games)

- Spot It! (Blue Orange Games)

- Guess Who? board game (Hasbro); note that manufacturer suggests that game is appropriate for ages 6 years and up, but 6-year-olds often need some help playing.

- Hedbanz Game (Spin Master Games); note that manufacturer suggests that game is appropriate for ages 7 or 8 years and up, but younger children can play easily with help.

- Go Fish (eeBoo or Imperial Kids); note that it is possible to play Go Fish with a standard set of playing cards but it is much easier to buy special Go Fish cards when playing with a young child.

- Other suggested games: Cranium, Super Story Recorder (like electronic Mad Libs), Battleship, Hangman

When possible, toys and games that were helpful with eliciting speech in the therapy room should be also used in the classroom to work on speech there.

Additional Exposure Exercises To Facilitate Speech with Various Individuals

- Play with voice changer toy (the toy alters the child's voice when spoken into).

- Have the child audio- or video-record himself and listen/watch with therapist or others (with very treatment-resistant children, you may consider having parent record child without telling them your purpose and then watch it with them without much forewarning; be careful not to ruin trust).

- Read to therapist (often easier than speaking), first from book and then in own words (e.g., child asking questions; see interview game).

- Interview game: Child and selected other individual (therapist at first) take turns asking each other questions about their "favorites" (e.g., ice cream, food, color, animal, game, vacation spot, etc.). With teacher or other individuals, this game can also include questions about simple pieces of personal information (e.g., middle name, number of siblings, etc).

- Popularity contest—like a survey: Using superheroes, sports, animals, colors, and so forth, create a chart and ask people (all peers in the class works particularly well) which are their favorites to see which one wins.

- Child makes beginning sounds of words and therapist guesses the words, or, similarly, child makes the sounds of words as if "sounding them out."

- Mouthing words: Ask child "this or that" questions and have child mouth answers. For example, "Which do you like better, dogs or cats?" "What would you rather have, a bunny or a duck?"

- Leave therapist message on answering machine/voice mail (assure child that you are not going to be answering). Repeat for teachers or others.

- Talk to therapist on walkie-talkie (or cell phone, although this is less novel).

- Practice lion roar for voice versus a whisper.

- Child may tolerate substituting "mmhmm" for a head nod as a step toward speaking (similarly, a sound for "no," and one for "I don't know"). If child can do this, follow up with silly game where answers are all Y, N, or IDK.

- Play animal guessing game with clues (like Twenty Questions, which can also be good). For example, the child thinks of an animal and the therapist (or other adult) asks a number of questions such as, "Is it an animal that I would feel safe to touch?" "Does it live in the water?"

- Child earns pennies (or finds them while playing the "hot and cold" game) and uses them to buy something at a real or pretend store (but with real prizes). Prompt child to ask how much items cost.

- For the child who has trouble with saying "hi" and "bye" (very common among children with SM), play a game where the child says "Hi" and "Bye" to the therapist over and over again. Children find this game rather amusing if the silliness is highlighted; walk toward each other and say "Hi," and then "Bye," and walk away. Immediately turn back and repeat in a different voice. Do this several times! This game is also helpful for children who have trouble saying "Thank you," which is also common and can be practiced while handing the child objects from the office. Last, child can practice with giving information like name, age, and the like. After mastering these tasks in session, child can be assigned to practice the same tasks out of session.

- Child takes food orders from others and goes to pretend bakery/ candy store and buys snacks for others. Children usually have the most fun with this when they "buy" real snacks or when they go to a real store (obviously only possible if one is nearby office).

- Child and therapist have contest to see how many of a category they each can each list (e.g., body parts, animals, etc.).

As mentioned throughout manual, exercises that are successful with therapists should be repeated with teachers or others with whom the child is having difficulty speaking.

Appendix B: Pretreatment Materials

Contents

School Speech Questionnaire*

Name of Teacher Who Completed This Questionnaire:

When responding to the following items, please consider the behavior of your student, _____, and activities of the past month and rate how often each statement is true.

1. When appropriate, this student talks to most peers at school.

       Always   Often   Seldom   Never

2. When appropriate, this student talks to selected peers (his/her friends) at school.

       Always   Often   Seldom   Never

3. When called on by his/her teacher, this student answers verbally.

       Always   Often   Seldom   Never

4. When appropriate, this student asks you (the teacher) questions.

       Always   Often   Seldom   Never

5. When appropriate, this student speaks to most teachers or staff at school.

       Always   Often   Seldom   Never

6. When appropriate, this student speaks in groups or in front of the class.

       Always   Often   Seldom   Never

*7. When appropriate, this student participates nonverbally in class (i.e., points, gestures, writes notes).

       Always   Often   Seldom   Never

*8. How much does not talking interfere with school for this student?

       Not at all   Slightly   Moderately   Extremely

Scoring: Always = 3, Often = 2, Seldom = 1, Never = 0

* These items are not included in total score.

Please consider your child's behavior in the last two weeks and rate how frequently each statement is true for your child.

AT SCHOOL

1. When appropriate, my child talks to most peers at school.

   Always   Often   Seldom   Never

2. When appropriate, my child talks to selected peers (his/her friends) at school.

   Always   Often   Seldom   Never

3. When my child is asked a question by his/her teacher, s/he answers.

   Always   Often   Seldom   Never

4. When appropriate, my child asks his or her teacher questions.

   Always   Often   Seldom   Never

5. When appropriate, my child speaks to most teachers or staff at school.

   Always   Often   Seldom   Never

6. When appropriate, my child speaks in groups or in front of the class.

   Always   Often   Seldom   Never

HOME/FAMILY

7. When appropriate, my child talks to family members living at home when other people are present.

   Always   Often   Seldom   Never

8. When appropriate, my child talks to family members while in unfamiliar places.

   Always   Often   Seldom   Never

9. When appropriate, my child talks to family members that don't live with him/her (e.g., grandparent, cousin).

   Always   Often   Seldom   Never

10. When appropriate, my child talks on the phone to his/her parents and siblings.

> Always   Often   Seldom   Never

11. When appropriate, my child speaks with family friends who are well-known to him/her.

> Always   Often   Seldom   Never

12. My child speaks to at least one babysitter.

> Always   Often   Seldom   Never N/A

IN SOCIAL SITUATIONS (OUTSIDE OF SCHOOL)

13. When appropriate, my child speaks with other children who s/he doesn't know.

> Always   Often   Seldom   Never

14. When appropriate, my child speaks with family friends who s/he doesn't know.

> Always   Often   Seldom   Never

15. When appropriate, my child speaks with his or her doctor and/or dentist.

> Always   Often   Seldom   Never

16. When appropriate, my child speaks to store clerks and/or waiters.

> Always   Often   Seldom   Never

17. When appropriate, my child talks when in clubs, teams, or organized activities outside of school.

> Always   Often   Seldom   Never N/A

Interference/Distress*

18. How much does not talking interfere with school for your child?

> Not at all   Slightly   Moderately   Extremely

19. How much does not talking interfere with family relationships?

> Not at all   Slightly   Moderately   Extremely

20. How much does not talking interfere in social situations for your child?

> Not at all   Slightly   Moderately   Extremely

21. Overall, how much does not talking interfere with life for your child?

> Not at all   Slightly   Moderately   Extremely

22. Overall, how much does not talking bother your child?

       Not at all   Slightly   Moderately Extremely

23. Overall, how much does your child's not talking bother you?

       Not at all   Slightly   Moderately Extremely

Scoring: Always = 3; Often = 2; Seldom = 1; Never = 0

*These items are not included in total score and are for clinical purposes only.

Copyright © 2008 R. Lindsey Bergman, Ph.D., Associate Clinical Professor, UCLA Semel Institute for Neuroscience and Human Behavior

R. Lindsey Bergman, Ph.D., Associate Clinical Professor, UCLA Semel Institute for Neuroscience and Human Behavior

Selective Mutism (SM) is a poorly understood and impairing condition in which a child fails to speak in certain social situations despite speaking regularly and normally in other situations. Most commonly, the child speaks normally at home with his/her family but does not speak at school or other places. Although in the past it was thought that SM was related to autism, oppositional defiant disorder, or trauma/abuse, most researchers now agree that SM is a form of social anxiety. This means that the failure to speak is related to feeling extremely shy, self-conscious, or embarrassed. Children with SM sometimes say that they are afraid that they will say something "dumb," or that their voice sounds "funny." Other children with SM may not be able to explain why they do not want to talk outside of their homes. The reluctance to speak is not due to not knowing the language or how to speak.

The onset of SM usually occurs before age 5, although it is often not identified or considered a problem until the child enters kindergarten. SM seems to be more common in girls than in boys. SM is considered a somewhat rare condition, although not as rare as was previously believed. Recent studies indicate that the prevalence of this condition is just under 1% of 5- to 7-year old children. It is important to consider that SM is probably no more rare than autism or obsessive compulsive disorder, two other childhood disorders.

Some people believe that SM is related to speech or language dysfunction, but recent studies have shown that most children with SM have normal language abilities. The causes of SM are not completely clear. However, the finding that social anxiety tends to run in the families of children with SM suggests that there could be a genetic component. Some researchers believe that SM is related to a general tendency to be shy and inhibited. SM does not appear to be related to the occurrence of a traumatic event in the child's life.

School is often difficult for the child with SM, who may fall behind socially or academically, or simply not get as much out of the experience as they would if they were speaking. Furthermore, school personnel do not always know how to respond to the lack of speech and can become punitive. Unfortunately, many people frequently assume that the child is merely being uncooperative and stubborn, has a language problem, or has severe emotional or intellectual disabilities. As a result, inappropriate placement in special classes or numerous failed attempts at intelligence testing may occur. Although children with SM who do not have speech or language problems do not need speech therapy, if speech therapy is delivered in a small-group format, it can be beneficial in that the smaller group may be an easier setting for working on speaking.

For some parents, living with a child who has SM can be extremely frustrating. The parents know that the child can speak normally and it feels as if the child is merely choosing not to. Attempts to "force" the child to speak are painful and unsuccessful, but ignoring the problem also seems harmful. Although experts now know that SM does not seem to be related to trauma or abuse, many people still believe this and may accuse parents of abusing their child. Attempts to educate others about SM may help with this issue.

Sometimes a failure to speak is present during the first few weeks of school and then a child begins talking on his or her own. Other times treatment is required. Unfortunately, it is difficult to predict which children will require treatment and which ones will not. The most effective treatments for SM are medication and cognitive behavioral therapy (CBT). The types of medication that are effective are selective serotonin reuptake inhibitors (SSRIs) such as Prozac or Luvox. CBT is a very focused and structured form of psychotherapy in which small and increasingly more difficult steps towards speaking are practiced and rewarded. CBT requires a substantial effort on the part of both the family affected by SM and individuals in the school setting.

Dear (principal),

I am currently treating *(child),* a student in *(teacher)*'s class, for Selective Mutism (SM).

As you may or may not be aware, SM is defined as a persistent failure to speak in specific situations (most commonly school) despite speaking in other situations (e.g., home). Most research links SM to severe social anxiety and suggests that early intervention is beneficial. Without intervention, it is difficult to assess academic progress among children with SM, and appropriate peer skills fail to develop.

SM is a problem that primarily manifests at school and our experience has indicated that teacher participation is vital to the success of the treatment. We and *(child)*'s parents are hoping that (teacher) will be interested in helping in the collaborative treatment team that we are building to help *(child)*. Typically, to implement school-related interventions, teachers spend a few minutes with the child at times when few or no other children are present (e.g., before class, during recess, after school).

One of the reasons for contacting you as the principal, is that early in treatment, it is often helpful to work with the child to "desensitize" them to the school environment in a low-stress situation. For instance, when a child is able to spend time in an empty classroom with just their parent, they are able to build calm associations with the classroom that they would otherwise never have the opportunity to build. I am hoping that it will be possible for *(child)* and parents to have access to the empty classroom as well as other school buildings on a very limited basis for these early stages of treatment.

Please feel free to get in touch with me should you have any questions about the treatment of SM or any other concerns.

Best,

Dear (teacher),

As you no doubt have noticed, your student, *(child)*, does not speak inside your classroom even though *(child)*'s speech is fluent and age appropriate at home. I have diagnosed *(child)* with Selective Mutism (SM) and she/he and her/his family are beginning treatment with me for this problem.

As you may or may not be aware, SM is defined as a persistent failure to speak in specific situations (most commonly school) despite speaking in other situations (e.g., home). Most research links SM to severe social anxiety and suggests that early intervention is beneficial. SM is a problem that primarily manifests at school and treatment experience has indicated that teacher participation is vital to the success of the treatment. Both myself and *(child)*'s parents (_____ and _____) are hoping that you will join us as a primary participant of a collaborative treatment team.

The treatment involves behavioral interventions focused on gradual exposure to difficult speaking situations. Your initial participation will entail providing information about your classroom and communicating your observations of *(child)*'s behavior. Then, as we together develop speaking assignments, your participation in implementing interventions and communicating their outcomes will be central to the treatment. Typically, school-related interventions involve the teacher spending a few minutes with the child at times when no other children are present (e.g., before class, during recess, after school). We ask that you implement the exposure situations exactly as assigned. This is important because even minor changes can alter the difficulty of the assignment for *(child)*. For instance, if *(child)*'s treatment has progressed to where she/he can tolerate speaking in private to you (without other children around), it is not likely to be successful if she/he were to attempt an assignment at that point with the other children in sight. We will use a binder or a notebook, passed back and forth between us, to communicate the nature of these assignments and their outcomes. At times, however, e-mail communication will probably be necessary, so I am hoping that you are willing to communicate via e-mail with me. My email address is _____. My phone number is:_____.

Before beginning treatment we need to assess how much speaking *(child)* does in the classroom. We have included a short questionnaire regarding speech in the classroom that we hope you can complete; it should not take more than 2 or 3 minutes.

As you can see, your participation in the treatment is essential. As such, the constraints on your time are one of my primary considerations and I will attempt to limit what I ask of you. I look forward to a positive and rewarding experience working with you as together, with the parents, we help *(child)* to speak more frequently in class and elsewhere. I urge you to please contact me whenever and as frequently as you may need to for clarification regarding assignments or to update me regarding progress.

Sincerely,

Appendix C: Treatment Forms

Contents

WEEKLY HOMEWORK FORM

CHILD: _____   THERAPIST: _____

THERAPIST CONTACT INFO: _____

DATE ASSIGNED: _____   → SESSION NUMBER: _____

ASSIGNMENT DESCRIPTION

Assignment #1: _____

_____

Assignment #2: _____

_____

Assignment #3: _____

_____

Assignment #4: _____

_____

COMMENTS: _____

_____

_____

_____

Please contact the therapist if you need any instructions of clarification.

PRIZE BRAINSTORMING FORM

Small Prizes	Medium Prizes	Large Prizes

FEELINGS CHART

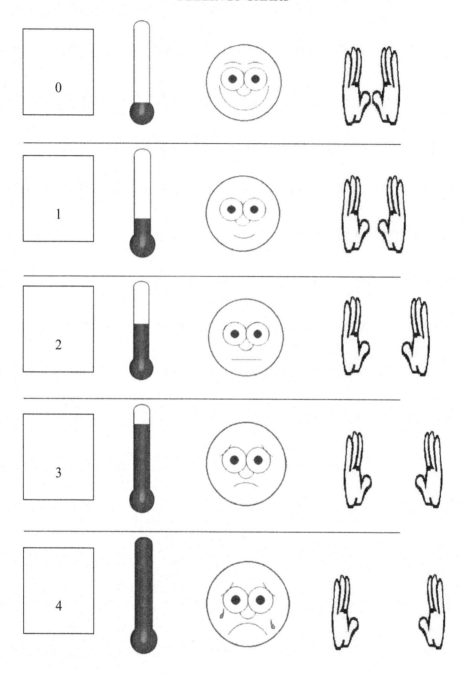

SITUATION RATING FORM

Instructions: Describe specific situations and how difficult they are. Some of these situations should NOT include speaking and should be very easy situations so that this task is not overwhelming. Others should be speaking situations.

EASY:

Situation: _____

Situation: _____

Situation: _____

MEDIUM:

Situation: _____

Situation: _____

Situation: _____

HARD:

Situation: _____

Situation: _____

Situation: _____

Instructions: List situations to work on, with the easiest situations at the bottom of the ladder and the hardest situations at the top.

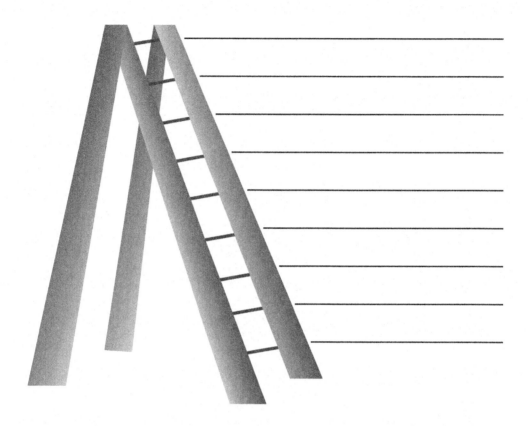

PLAYDATE FORM

Date: _____ Parent-Observer: _____

Individuals Present: _____

Difficulty rating:_____ Setting: _____

Activities: _____

_____

Parent Observations (record both verbal and nonverbal behavior):

_____

_____

_____

_____

_____

_____

_____

_____

_____

_____

_____

_____

_____

_____

_____

CLASSMATE LIST

Instructions: Use this form to list the names of other children in class or program with your child. If child has trouble with one gender more than the other, please list them separately.

Name:_____M/F   Name:_____M/F

Name:_____M/F   Name:_____M/F

Name:_____M/F   Name:_____M/F

Name:_____M/F   Name:_____M/F

Name:_____M/F   Name:_____M/F

Name:_____M/F   Name:_____M/F

Name:_____M/F   Name:_____M/F

Name:_____M/F   Name:_____M/F

Name:_____M/F   Name:_____M/F

Name:_____M/F   Name:_____M/F

Name:_____M/F   Name:_____M/F

Name:_____M/F   Name:_____M/F

Name:_____M/F   Name:_____M/F

Name:_____M/F   Name:_____M/F

Name:_____M/F   Name:_____M/F

CLASS CHART

Child's Name	Description of Speech	Where Speech Has Occurred	Quality of Speech	Playdate?	Spoken To Child's Parents?

EXPOSURE ASSIGNMENT FORM

CHILD: _____ PARENTS: _____

Exposure with (circle one)

    TEACHER:_____PARENT:_____OTHER:_____

DATE ASSIGNED: ____/____/____ → SESSION NUMBER: _____

ASSIGNMENT DESCRIPTION

a) Assignment: _____

_____

b) Reward expected: _____

_____

****

PARENT/TEACHER, PLEASE RECORD OUTCOME: O COMPLETED

                                        O NOT COMPLETED

Please Describe Outcome of Assignment _____

_____

_____

_____

_____

Therapist Notes on Assignment

c) **Outcome of assignment:**   O Not attempted—not possible

                                   O Not attempted—child did not tolerate

                                   O Attempted not completed

                                   O Completed as assigned

                                   O Completed with modification

        Child's feeling rating after exposure: ☺   ☺   ☺   ☹   ☹

        Check here _____ if child rating not obtained

Explain outcome: _____

_____

_____

_____

Other Individuals List

Use this form to list the children that your child knows from extracurricular activities outside of school and other adults that your child interacts with outside of school. They can be listed by name or type of person if adult (e.g., hairdresser, waiter).

CHILDREN: **ADULTS:**

_____M/F   _____M/F

_____M/F   _____M/F

_____M/F   _____M/F

_____M/F   _____M/F

_____M/F   _____M/F

_____M/F   _____M/F

_____M/F   _____M/F

_____M/F   _____M/F

_____M/F   _____M/F

_____M/F   _____M/F

_____M/F   _____M/F

_____M/F   _____M/F

_____M/F   _____M/F

_____M/F   _____M/F

_____M/F   _____M/F

OTHER INDIVIDUALS CHART

Individual's Name	Description of Individual	Description of Speech	Quality of Speech	Normal Spontaneous Speech?

Exposure Ideas Form

CHILD: _____ PARENTS: _____ TEACHER: _____

Date assigned: _____/_____/_____

- -

General Areas of Remaining Difficulty:

_____

_____

_____

_____

_____

_____

_____

_____

_____

_____

Specific Ideas for Exposures:

_____

_____

_____

_____

_____

_____

_____

_____

_____

_____

_____

PROGRESS CHART: _____ ACCOMPLISHMENTS!

Instructions: Use the space below to record the child's progress, for example, categories might include classmates, other kids, teachers, family members, or other adults.

Category (fill-in):

- _____
- _____
- _____

Category (fill-in):

- _____
- _____
- _____

Category (fill-in):

- _____
- _____
- _____

Category (fill-in):

- _____
- _____
- _____

Category (fill-in):

- _____
- _____
- _____

REMAINING GOALS WORKSHEET

GOAL	EXPOSURES	REWARD

Certificate of Achievement

This certificate is presented to

_____

for successful completion of the
Talking Program

_____

References

American Psychiatric Association. (2000). *Diagnostic and statistical manual of mental disorders* (4th ed., text rev.). Washington, DC: Author.

Beidel, D. C., Turner, S. M., & Morris, T. L. (2000). Behavioral treatment of childhood social phobia. *Journal of Consulting and Clinical Psychology, 68*, 1072–1080.

Bergman, R. L., & Lee, J. C. (2009). Selective mutism. In B. J. Sadock, V. A. Sadock, & P. Ruiz (Eds.), *Kaplan and Sadock's comprehensive textbook of psychiatry* (9th ed., Vol. 1., pp. 3694–3699). Philadelphia: Lippincott Williams & Wilkins.

Bergman, R. L., Piacentini, J., & McCracken, J. T. (2002). Prevalence and description of selective mutism in a school-based sample. *Journal of the American Academy of Child and Adolescent Psychiatry, 41*(8), 938–946.

Black, B., & Uhde, T. W. (1994). Treatment of elective mutism with fluoxetine: A double-blind, placebo-controlled study. *Journal of the American Academy of Child and Adolescent Psychiatry, 33*, 1000–1006.

Black, B., & Uhde, T. W. (1995). Psychiatric characteristics of children with selective mutism: A pilot study. *Journal of the American Academy of Child and Adolescent Psychiatry, 34*(7), 847–856.

Blum, N. J., Kell, R. S., Starr, H. L., Lender, W. L., Bradley- Klug, K. L., Osborne, M. L., & Dowrick, P. W. (1998). Case study: Audio feedforward treatment of selective mutism. *Journal of the American Academy of Child and Adolescent Psychiatry, 37*(1), 40–43.

Carlson, J. S., Mitchell, A. D., & Segool, N. (2008). The current state of empirical support for the pharmacological treatment of selective mutism. *Michigan State University School Psychology Quarterly, 23*(3), 354–372.

Cleave, H. (2009). Too anxious to speak? The implications of current research into selective mutism for educational psychology practice. *Educational Psychology in Practice, 25*(3), 233–246.

Cohan, S. L., Chavira, D. A., & Stein, M. B. (2006). Practitioner review: Psychosocial interventions for children with selective mutism: A critical evaluation of the literature from 1990–2005. *Journal of Child Psychology and Psychiatry and Allied Disciplines, 47*(11), 1085–1097.

Dow, S. P., Sonies, B. C., Scheib, D., Moss, S. E., Leonard, H. L. (1995). Practical guidelines for the assessment and treatment of selective mutism. *Journal of the American Academy of Child and Adolescent Psychiatry, 34*(7), 836–846.

Dummit, E. S., Klein, R. G., Tancer, N. K., Asche, B., Martin, J. (1996). Fluoxetine treatment of children with selective mutism: An open trial. *Journal of the American Academy of Child and Adolescent Psychiatry, 35,* 615–621.

Dummit, E. S., Klein, R. G., Tancer, N. K., Asche, B., Martin, J. (1997). Systematic assessment of 50 children with selective mutism. *Journal of the American Academy of Child and Adolescent Psychiatry, 36*(5), 653–660.

Elizur, Y., & Perednik, R. (2003). Prevalence and description of selective mutism in immigrant and native families: A controlled study. *Journal of the American Academy of Child and Adolescent Psychiatry, 42,* 1451–1459.

Guy, W. (1976). *ECDEU assessment manual for psychopharmacology, revised* (218–222). Rockville, MD: National Institute of Mental Health.

Kearney, C. A., Haight, C., & Day, T. L. (2011). Selective mutism. In D. McKay & E. Storch (Eds.), *Handbook of child and adolescent anxiety disorders* (pp. 275–287). New York: Springer.

Wendy K. Silverman, William M. Kurtines – 1996–142 p. *Anxiety and Phobic Disorders: A Pragmatic Approach.* Plenum Press New York.

Kehle, T. J., Owen, S. V., & Cressy, E. T. (1990). The use of self-modeling as an intervention in school psychology: A case study of an elective mute. *School Psychology Review, 19,* 115–121.

Kendall, P. C. (1994). Treating anxiety disorders in children: Results of a randomized clinical trial. *Journal of Consulting and Clinical Psychology, 62*(1), 100–110.

Kendall, P. C., & Hedtke, K. A. (2006). *Cognitive-behavioral therapy for anxious children: Therapist manual* (3rd ed.). Ardmore, PA: Workbook Publishing.

Koeppen, A .S. (1974). Relaxation training for children. *Elementary School Guidance and Counseling, 9,* 14–21.

Krohn, D. D., Weckstein, S. M., & Wright, H. L. (1992). A study of the effectiveness of a specific treatment for elective mutism. *Journal of the American Academy of Child and Adolescent Psychiatry, 31,* 711–718.

Lang, R., Regester, A., Mulloy, A., Rispoli, M., & Botout, A. (2011). Behavioral intervention to treat selective mutism across multiple social situations and community settings. *Journal of Applied Behavior Analysis, 44*(3), 623–628.

Manassis, K., & Tannock, R. (2008). Comparing interventions for selective mutism: A pilot study. *Canadian Journal of Psychiatry, 53*(10), 700–703.

Manassis, K., Tannock, R., Garland, E. J., Minde, K., & McInnes, A. (2007). The sounds of silence: Language, cognition, and anxiety in selective mutism. *Journal of the American Academy of Child and Adolescent Psychiatry, 46*(9), 1187–1195.

Masten, W. G., Stacks, J. R., Caldwell- Colbert, A. T., & Jackson, J. S. (1996). Behavioral treatment of a selectively mute Mexican-American boy. *Psychology in the Schools, 33*, 56–60.

Ollendick, T. H., & Cerny, J. A. (1981). *Clinical behaviour therapy with children.* New York: Plenum Press.

Piacentini, J. C., Langley, A., & Roblek, T. (2007). *It's only a false alarm: A cognitive-behavioral treatment program—Therapist guide.* New York: Oxford University Press.

Porjes, M. D. (1992). Intervention with the selectively mute child. *Psychology in the Schools, 29*, 367–376.

The Research Unit on Pediatric Psychopharmacology Anxiety Study Group. (2001). RUPP: Fluvoxamine for the treatment of anxiety disorders in children and adolescents. *The New England Journal of Medicine, 344*, 1279–1285.

Richburg, M. L., & Cobia, D. C. (1994). Using behavioral techniques to treat elective mutism: A case study. *Elementary School Guidance and Counseling, 28*(3), 214–219.

Rye, M. S., & Ullman, D. (1999). The successful treatment of long-term selective mutism: A case study. *Journal of Behavior Therapy and Experimental Psychiatry, 30*, 313–323.

Sharkey, L., McNicholas, F., Barry, E., Begley, M., & Ahern, S. (2008). Group therapy for selective mutism: A parents' and children's treatment group. *Journal of Behavior Therapy and Experimental Psychiatry, 39*(4), 538–545.

Silverman, W. K., & Albano, A. M. (1996). *The Anxiety Disorders Interview Schedule for Children for DSM-IV: Child and parent versions.* San Antonio, TX: Psychological Corporation.

Spence, S. H., Donovan, C., & Brechman-Toussaint, M. (2000). The treatment of childhood social phobia: The effectiveness of a social skills training-based, cognitive behavioural intervention, with and without parental involvement. *The Journal of Child Psychology and Psychiatry, 41,* 713–726.

Steinhausen, H. S., Wachter, M., Laimbock, K., & Metzke, C. W. (2006). A long-term outcome study of selective mutism in childhood. *The Journal of Child Psychology and Psychiatry, 47*(7), 751–756.

Vecchio J. L., & Kearney, C. A. (2005). Selective mutism in children: Comparison to youths with and without anxiety disorders. *Journal of Psychopathology & Behavioral Assessment, 27,* 31–37.

Vecchio, J. L., & Kearney, C. A. (2009). Treating youths with selective mutism with an alternating design of exposure-based practice and contingency management. *Behavior Therapy Journal, 40,* 380–392.

Viana, A. G., Beidel, D. C., & Rabian, B. (2009). Selective mutism: A review and integration of the last 15 years. *Clinical Psychology Review, 29*(1), 57–67.

Watson, T. S., & Kramer, J. J. (1992). Multimethod behavioral treatment of long-term selective mutism. *Psychology in the Schools, 29,* 359–365

Wright, H. H., Cuccaro, M. L., Leonhardt, T. V., Kendall, D. F., & Anderson, J. H. (1995). Case study: Fluoxetine in the multimodal treatment of a preschool child with selective mutism. *Journal of the American Academy of Child and Adolescent Psychiatry, 34*(7), 857–862.

About the Author

R. Lindsey Bergman, Ph.D., is Associate Clinical Professor of Psychiatry and Biobehavioral Sciences in the David Geffen School of Medicine and Associate Director of the UCLA Child OCD and Anxiety Program. She is also Director of the Pediatric OCD Intensive Outpatient Program at the Resnick Neuropsychiatric Hospital at UCLA. Dr. Bergman received her Ph.D. in Clinical Psychology from UCLA in 1995 and joined the newly established UCLA Child OCD Program shortly thereafter. She was the recipient of a treatment development award from the National Institute of Mental Health to establish a manualized treatment for selective mutism. Clinically, Dr. Bergman specializes in cognitive behavioral treatment (CBT) for children and adolescents with selective mutism, OCD, and related disorders. Her empirical work seeks to further understand, develop, and test CBT and other evidence-based interventions available to anxious children. Dr. Bergman has received several research awards to study the treatment of childhood anxiety, and she has served as co-investigator on several treatment outcome studies. She is a committed CBT supervisor and teacher for both psychology and psychiatry trainees at UCLA.

CPSIA information can be obtained
at www.ICGtesting.com
Printed in the USA
BVOW03s2133041216
469540BV00008B/6/P